Neighborhood Groups

and

Urban Renewal

Number Five: Metropolitan Politics Series

Neighborhood Groups
and
Urban Renewal

By J. Clarence Davies, III

COLUMBIA UNIVERSITY PRESS
New York and London 1966

Clarence J. Davies, III, is Budget Examiner for Environmental Health, Bureau of the Budget, Executive Office of the President. He was formerly Director of the Bureau of Municipal Research at Bowdoin College.

To Barbara

Preface

This study, like most of the other volumes of the Metropolitan Politics Series, was originally a Columbia University doctoral dissertation. It has gone through several revisions since its appearance as a dissertation, and I hope for the reader's sake that the scars of its genesis are not too obvious.

In conducting the research for the dissertation I interviewed more than seventy-five persons, most of whom prefer to remain anonymous. Those interviewed were mostly neighborhood leaders, but government officials and other informed observers were also included. I owe a debt of gratitude to all of these people for giving freely of their time (some of the interviews lasted four or five hours) and knowledge. This study would have been impossible without their cooperation. Thanks are also due to the New York Housing and Redevelopment Board, the New York City Planning Commission, the Commission on Human Relations, the Citizens Housing and Planning Council, and Stryckers Bay Neighborhood Council for the use of their files.

My personal and intellectual indebtedness to Professor Wallace S. Sayre, who served as my adviser throughout the Ph.D. process, is great. Whether acting as counselor, antagonist, or source of wisdom, he remained always a fine teacher. He has left his imprint not only on this manuscript but on my entire approach to political matters. The same may be said of Professor David B. Truman, now Dean of Columbia College. I will always be thankful that I arrived at Columbia before his departure from the teaching world.

While at Columbia my working world consisted primarily of my colleagues on the Metropolitan Region Program. Although I am thankful to the Ford Foundation for its monetary help, I am even more grateful to it for having brought together the small group of would-be political scientists who made up "the Program." The Program headquarters at 605 West 115th Street did not physically resemble a medieval university (except, perhaps, in age), but the venerable tradition of a community of scholars and friends was maintained, and I do not think that any of us will forget the excitement of the experience.

A word should be said about the propriety of writing an empirical study of events in which one's father was an important actor. I believe that I have overcome any bias resulting from his involvement, but this must be left to the reader to judge. I do owe my interest in urban renewal in great part to my father's interest. While our views of both urban renewal and neighborhood groups differ, he has been of invaluable assistance in this entire project. His kindness and tolerance toward his academic offspring, who was reviewing the past events of his career with the benefit of hindsight and without the burden of responsibility, has never flagged. While I know that he will not agree with much in this study, I hope that it will please him.

Thanks are due to the Ford Foundation for giving me the means to obtain food and shelter while in graduate school and for making this publication possible. Bernard Gronert of the Columbia University Press was most helpful in initiating me into the mysteries of the publishing world. Katherine M. Purcell served as a wise and skillful editor of the manuscript.

Despite my indebtedness to so many people, the usual disclaimer must be made. The sole responsibility for anything contained in this study rests, for better or worse, with the author.

Bowdoin College   J. CLARENCE DAVIES, III
Brunswick, Maine
June, 1965

Contents

Metropolitan Politics Series

This is the fifth in the series of books resulting from the metropolitan study program begun at Columbia University in 1957 and supported by a grant from the Ford Foundation.

The faculty committee supervising this program and serving as editors of the series are Wallace S. Sayre, Chairman, Richard E. Neustadt and David B. Truman of the Department of Public Law and Government of Columbia University, and William N. Cassella, Jr., of the National Municipal League.

Abbreviations of Agencies and Organizations

CCGNY	Community Council of Greater New York
CHPC	Citizens Housing and Planning Council
COIR	Commission on Intergroup Relations
CPC	City Planning Commission
CSWV	Committee to Save the West Village
FHA	Federal Housing Administration
GVA	Greenwich Village Association
HHFA	Housing and Home Finance Agency
HRB	Housing and Redevelopment Board
Micove	Middle Income Co-operators of Greenwich Village
NAACP	National Association for the Advancement of Colored People
SCC	Slum Clearance Committee
VID	Village Independent Democrats
WSURA	West Side Urban Renewal Area
WVC	West Village Council

Neighborhood Groups

and

Urban Renewal

CHAPTER I

Introduction

When the National Housing Act of 1949 was passed, urban renewal was hailed as the tool that would enable the cities of America to save themselves from blight, decay, and obsolescence. Since 1949 the obstacles that can impede the execution of a successful urban renewal program have become apparent. The effort to revitalize the nation's cities has raised numerous problems not anticipated when the Housing Act became law.[1] Of these obstacles and problems, none has raised more questions and caused more controversy than the role to be played by the groups of residents on or near the site of a proposed renewal project. This study is an attempt to explore the behavior of such groups.

The primary concern of the study is with neighborhood groups as political interest groups, in other words, as organized groups of individuals making demands upon the government.[2] A large body of political science literature deals with interest groups and the role they play in the political process at all levels.[3] I have tried to contribute to this literature by examining how groups become involved in a controversy and how they are able to influence government officials. In examining how groups become involved, one is also led to a consideration of the kinds of stakes that will spur individuals and groups into taking political action.

In examining these questions, I have been somewhat eclectic in choosing a general framework. The basic research orientation is drawn from two sources: Sayre and Kaufman's *Governing New York City* [4] and Truman's *The Governmental Process*. Following Truman, I have focused primarily on group rather than individual activity. I have also adopted the concept of "access" as being the goal for which all political-interest groups strive. From Sayre and Kaufman I have incorporated the general idea of a political process consisting of actors who work within a set of rules to defend certain stakes or to get certain rewards by influencing the actions of government officials.

The political aspects of housing and urban renewal have been the subject of a number of studies in recent years. Meyerson and Banfield studied the political dynamics of the location of public housing projects in Chicago.[5] Their examination of the "climate of neighborhood opinion" [6] illustrates the kinds of stakes that neighborhood residents may have in an area and the dominant role played by factors of race in the Chicago setting. Dahl has showed how a dynamic mayor could mobilize the political forces in New Haven to support a massive program of urban renewal.[7] The first volume in the Metropolitan Politics Series, Kaplan's study of Newark, N.J., also showed the kinds of political strategy necessary to gain approval for large-scale renewal projects.[8] In Newark, neighborhood opposition was "insignificant." [9] The one instance of neighborhood revolt against a project was sparked primarily by aspirants for political office.[10] Gans has described how opposition to a renewal project in Boston's West End failed to materialize because of the cultural attributes of the neighborhood residents.[11] Rossi and Dentler studied the stages of community organization in the Hyde Park-Kenwood renewal area in Chicago.[12] The neighborhood groups in the area were eventually overshadowed by the University of Chicago, which played a dominant part in the renewal process.

None of the above studies examined New York, and none of them seemed to describe the kind of renewal controversies that have taken place in New York in recent years. Therefore, I undertook three case studies to determine the role neighborhood groups have played in urban renewal in New York. The limitations inherent in trying to base generalizations upon three cases in one city are obvious, but the existing literature on interest groups, on urban neighborhoods, and on urban renewal has provided a guide against which to check the hypotheses developed from the cases. An attempt was also made to consider the widest possible range of cases in the belief that any generalizations would have to be tested against renewal proposals that differed as much from each other as possible. The aspects of each proposal considered most important in choosing the cases were (1) the agency that initiated the proposal, (2) the type of area in which the project was to be located, and (3) the degree and outcome of the controversy about the project.

The first case, Seaside-Hammels, actually consisted of two projects, but the projects were administered by the city as one and were located quite close to each other. Both projects were initiated by the Mayor's Committee on Slum Clearance at about the same time (late 1953 and early 1954). The Seaside site contained only a small number of people, most of them homeowners. The Hammels site was occupied by a large community of low-income Negroes. The surrounding area had a white population of mixed ethnic origin and a wide range of incomes. The controversy over the projects never became citywide, and few alterations in the project plans seemed to be due to community pressure.

The West Village urban renewal project, the subject of the second case study, was initiated in 1961 by the newly formed Housing and Redevelopment Board (HRB). The site for the proposed project included a population that was mixed both ethnically and economically, although it was predominantly white. The battle against HRB's application for planning and survey funds became a major city issue. The neighborhood groups combatting the application were successful, and the possibility that any project would be built was destroyed before the plans had been drawn.

The proposal for the West Side Urban Renewal Area, (WSURA), the third case study, was initiated in 1955, although the controversy did not come to a head until 1962. The plan was under the supervision of the Urban Renewal Board until 1961, when it was taken over by HRB. The site area included a large number of Puerto Ricans. The project represented the first major attempt by the city to encourage local citizen participation in the renewal process. There was a high degree of controversy over the project, and major changes were made in the final plans to conform more nearly to the desires of some of the neighborhood groups.

The three areas studied are typical of New York in that they are largely composed of ethnic minorities and lack a high degree of homogeneity. It should be noted, however, that some important segments of the New York population did not play a central role in the cases. A few Italian groups were active in Seaside-Hammels, and there were small Irish communities in the West Village and the West Side, but both these ethnic grops are underrepresented in the cases. Also, none of the three areas was a "working-class" neighborhood. In each there was a significant proportion of middle-income residents, a fact that may have led to increased interest-group activity.[13]

The three cases form the factual core of this study. They will be preceded by a chapter on the general background and political setting of urban renewal in New York. Following the cases come three chapters of analysis. Chapter VI tries to explain why different groups and individuals take different stands on an urban renewal proposal. It describes the stakes that individuals have in renewal and the more general factors that influence group attitudes. Chapter VII explores why existing neighborhood groups either were or were not active in the renewal controversy, why *ad hoc* groups were formed, and why nonneighborhood groups became involved in the renewal controversies. The attitudes of neighborhood residents are politically signifi-cant primarily in so far as they find organized expression through groups. We must thus try to account for which atti-tudes will find the most powerful expression. Chapter VIII ex-amines the different ways in which neighborhood groups can try to influence the government and the effects of the city's political structure on the role neighborhood groups play in urban re-newal. Finally, in Chapter IX, I attempt to determine whether neighborhood group participation in the urban renewal process contributes to the public interest.

CHAPTER II

Urban Renewal in New York City

WHAT IS URBAN RENEWAL?

At the end of World War II America's cities were faced with a serious housing problem. In most urban areas the supply of housing was inadequate. Much of the housing that did exist consisted of slum dwellings in bad condition and without many of the basic necessities for decent living. Each year the number of slum dwellings increased.

The cities' problems were not being met by the efforts of private builders. The cost of construction forced private developers to charge higher rents than most people could afford to pay. Public assistance of some sort was clearly called for.

There were several ways in which public resources could be used to meet the demands for middle- and low-income rental housing. The most obvious was for the government to build and operate its own projects. The rents of the tenants in such projects would be directly subsidized by the government. This approach had already been used during the Depression, and its use was to be continued after the war.

It was clear, however, that the dimensions of the housing problem in 1945 were so great that direct construction and operation by the government could not provide a total solution. It was politically unfeasible for the government to build and maintain all the housing that was needed. Some plan was necessary that would bring private developers into the tasks of constructing new housing at moderate rentals and of helping to remove the existing slums. The government would have to supply some sort of subsidy to make it possible for the developers to make a profit while charging rents that middle-income people could afford or while building in the less desirable areas where the slums were located.

Such a subsidy could take various forms. Three different proposals were given the most consideration: (1) a reduction in the taxes paid by the developer, (2) the provision of low-interest mortgages that would lower the amount the builder would have to pay to finance the construction, and (3) lowering the price that the developers would have to pay for the land on which the housing would be built. All three forms could potentially reduce the cost of building to make it feasible for a private company to build on slum sites and to charge lower rentals.

The National Housing Act of 1949 made low-interest mortgages available through the Federal Housing Administration. The Act relied primarily, however, on lowering the cost of land. Title I of the Act permits municipalities to condemn parcels of land and then to buy these parcels for the purpose of clearing slums. The municipality then resells the land at a lower price to a private developer, who agrees to construct a project on the site. Sometimes the municipality draws up the plans for the project, but most often the developer draws up plans that are subject to approval by both the federal and the local government. The federal government pays two-thirds of the difference between the price at which the land was bought by the municipality and the lower price at which it was resold to the developer. The local government pays the remaining third. In practice, the local government's share is often paid in the form of land already owned within the site or in public services of some sort rather than in actual cash.[1]

The 1949 Housing Act assumed that the land condemned for renewal would be totally cleared. In 1954 a new housing act was passed to provide for the possible conservation and rehabilitation of the buildings on the site. An alternative to the total-clearance "bulldozer" approach was thus given federal support.

Originally, the term "urban renewal" applied only to the Title I program outlined above. In common parlance, however, the term is often used to apply to all publicly aided housing programs, which in New York includes public housing consisting of low-rent projects built and owned by the City, often with federal or state assistance. It includes housing built under the New York State Mitchell-Lama Law, which combines use of condemnation for site assembly with low-interest mortgages and partial tax exemption for the new buildings. It also includes projects making use of Sec. 221(d)(3) of the Housing Act of 1961, which provides for a program of federal mortgage insurance and purchase aimed at increasing the supply of middle-income housing.[2]

In New York the politics of the Title I program have been complex. A wide variety of actors have played a role in the "urban renewal game." [3] The "rules of the game," [4] the stipulations of local, state, and federal law that govern the renewal process, have given a number of government bodies an important role in urban renewal (see Table 1). A project in New York must be initiated by the City's Housing and Redevelopment Board (HRB). An application for planning and survey funds must then be approved by the City Planning Commission (CPC) and by the Board of Estimate. The application is then submitted to the Housing and Home Finance Agency (HHFA) of the federal government, which must give its approval. (In practice, HRB often asks HHFA for unofficial approval before submitting plans to the Board of Estimate.) When the planning and survey funds are obtained and the plans for the project have been drawn, the whole process begins again with an application for funds for the purchase of the land. If this application is approved, the land is sold to a sponsor who has received the approval of the HRB and the Board of Estimate. The sponsor usually must try to get approval from the Federal Housing Administration (FHA) for a government-backed mortgage to help finance the project. Futhermore, any change in the project plans must again receive the official approval of CPC, the Board of Estimate, and HHFA.

TABLE 1. Major Governmental Actors in the Urban Renewal Process

Agency [a]	Membership	Functions [b]
Mayor's Committee on Slum Clearance (before May, 1960)	Chairman and vice-chairman appointed by Mayor and three members ex officio [c]	Conceives project, finds sponsor, requests planning, survey, and project funds
Housing and Redevelopment Board (after May, 1960)	Chairman and two members appointed by Mayor	Same as Committee on Slum Clearance
City Planning Commission	Chairman and six members appointed by Mayor [d]	Declares area blighted, approves requests for planning and project funds
Board of Estimate	Mayor, Comptroller, President of City Council, five Borough Presidents	Approves requests for planning and project funds
Housing and Home Finance Agency	Administrator appointed by President with advice and consent of Senate	Approves and grants requests for planning and project funds

[a] Includes only those agencies whose official approval is necessary for a project.
[b] Description of functions throughout table is simplified for the sake of clarity.
[c] Three additional members appointed by the Mayor, June, 1959.
[d] Before 1961, Chief Engineer of the Board of Estimate was a member ex officio.

Later in the chapter we shall discuss each of these governmental actors in the urban renewal game. It is useful, however, to note here that many nongovernmental actors also play a part in the urban renewal process. The major focus of this paper is on neighborhood groups, a catagory defined as including any organization whose interests or membership are less than borough-wide in scope. These organizations cannot be considered apart from the population characteristics of the neighborhood, and thus we shall also be concerned with ethnic and economic groupings, even if they are not formally organized.

Neighborhood groups usually become actors in the renewal game because a project is scheduled to be built or is actually built in the area of which they are a part. Some of these groups, the Committee to Save the West Village or the Gramercy Neighbors, for example, may have been formed for the specific purpose of playing a part in urban renewal. The many groups that already exist in most neighborhoods—the churches, the settlement houses, the P-TAs, the political clubs—are capable of becoming political-interest groups [5] in the urban renewal process if they feel that their interests are being directly affected.

Neighborhood groups are not the only nongovernmental actors in the urban renewal game. Members of occupational groups play a direct role in the renewal process—builders, architects, bankers, and real estate men. Many of these groups are strategically placed to influence the nature of the renewal program. The success of urban renewal is dependent upon the cooperation of builders and financiers, and if they withhold their support, the program is doomed to failure. But the degree of support they give may vary. The strong support of the city's financial community was one of the props upon which Robert Moses' strength rested. The HRB under J. Clarence Davies, Jr., was not hindered by lack of support from the financial community, but it did not receive the same sort of backing that had been given to Moses.

In addition to the occupational groups, other citywide groups become involved in renewal because of their ideological orientation or because some particular project affects the interest of a part of their membership. Such groups as the Citizens Housing and Planning Council (CHPC), NAACP, the Citizens Union, and the labor unions fall into this category. For some of these groups, concern with urban renewal is part of the purpose of the organization, and thus involvement in any renewal proposal is institutionalized. Thus, CHPC has a committee which considers every new renewal plan, and the reports of this committee are reviewed by the board of directors, which takes a stand for or against the plan. The Community Service Society has recently instituted a similar arrangement. Other citywide groups are drawn into the renewal process because of alliances with groups that become involved, because they see a chance to strengthen their internal organization by taking a stand, or because some aspect of the renewal process happens to touch upon a matter the organization considers vital to its reason for being. The mass media, particularly the city's newspapers, also play an important role in renewal controversies, a role that affects the behavior of most of the other groups. Later I shall describe in more detail how citywide groups become involved in urban renewal. I shall now turn to the governmental actors in the renewal process.

THE ADMINISTRATION OF URBAN RENEWAL IN NEW YORK CITY

The Slum Clearance Committee. Even before the final passage of the 1949 Housing Act, Mayor William O'Dwyer had set up a Slum Clearance Committee (SCC), designed to formulate and execute projects under the provisions of Title I. O'Dwyer appointed Robert Moses, already the dominant figure in New York public works projects, chairman of the committee. For the next ten years, SCC and the Title I program in New York were essentially the work of Moses. For all practical purposes he *was* SCC.

The exact bases of Moses' power have yet to be revealed.[6] For almost thirty years he has been the key figure behind most of the major public construction work in both the State and the City of New York. A Republican, he has been considered indispensable by Democratic governors and mayors. His wide variety of titles (he held twelve state and city posts in 1961) reflects the range of his influence and also contributes to his power. In the absence of any careful political analysis of Moses' career, one can perhaps isolate three factors that have been, at least in part, responsible for Moses' power—his personality, his strategic methods, and his staff.

Moses' personality can only be described as powerful. He is able to delegate authority and is a good administrator, but he is absolutely convinced of the correctness of his views and the wrong-headedness of his opponents.[7] A colleague of his described a "Moses Conference" in this way: "Moses opens the meeting, states the problem and his proposed solution: when objections are raised Moses calls them 'nonsense.' The meeting is then adjorned and Moses circulates a memo on the agreement that was reached." [8] Combine this self-assuredness with a keen intelligence capable of thinking on a vast scale, a sharp sense of timing, publicity, and political strategy, and a basically pragmatic outlook—and you have the almost ideal personality for an entrepreneur of public works.[9] Moses' vast experience has also given him an advantage in that he can speak from first-hand knowledge about matters with which most of his associates have only a vague familiarity.

Moses' pragmatism is the key element in his political strategy. During his chairmanship of SCC, all his energies were concentrated on the completion of his projects, and he was willing to use whatever means were available within the law to accomplish this end. He was undoubtedly aware that Democratic Party leaders were in a good position to obstruct the Title I program because of their influence on the Board of Estimate. Thus, many sponsors, appraisers, and relocaters who were given project work had close ties with the Party.

Moses and his staff claim that it was primarily the support of the business and financial community which helped them in their urban renewal efforts. They point to the assistance rendered by David Rockefeller's Downtown Lower Manhattan Association in obtaining several Title I projects in Manhattan. There is no doubt that the support of the business and financial community has contributed to Moses' success. One must also point to the support that the mass media have given to Moses and to the public image of him as a man who could get things done. Moses' past successes have given him a reputation leading to increased power and responsibility and thus to more success.[10]

Over the years Moses has collected a staff of highly skilled men who share his philosophy and are personally devoted to him. They are used on almost all the projects with which he is concerned. Most of this staff hold positions with the Triborough Bridge and Tunnel Authority, of which Moses is chairman. They receive salaries commensurate to those in private industry, and it is often said that their ability to gather information, both of a technical and a political nature, is far superior to that of any other local or state governmental agency.[11] Moses is thus often able to speak with a better knowledge of the facts in any given case than are his opponents or obstructors.

Between 1949 and 1959, SCC was organized as a typical Moses operation. The staff consisted almost entirely of Moses' men. George Spargo was assistant to the chairman, Samuel Brooks was the director, and William S. Lebwohl was the counsel. Spargo had been the general manager of the Triborough Bridge and Tunnel Authority since 1944, and Lebwohl was the Authority's counsel. Both continued to work for the Authority while they served with SCC. The vice-chairman of the committee, who had the key job of reporting on the financial qualifications of prospective sponsors, was Thomas Shanahan. Shanahan, the president of the Federation Bank and Trust Company and a man with close ties to the Democratic Party organization, was a good friend of Moses' and had worked with him on many other matters. The other members of the committee consisted of the chairman of CPC, the head of the Bureau (later a department) of Real Estate, and the Commissioner of Buildings. These three ex officio members were unable to make any independent evaluation of the decisions reached by Moses and his staff, because they were never informed about what Moses was going to do until it had already been done or was just about to be done. The meetings of SCC were merely an occasion for communicating decisions that had already been made.

Moses and his staff viewed the goals of the Title I program as twofold: to demolish slums and to increase the tax revenues of the city. Aspects of the program that did not fall within these two goals, such as relocation and the nature of the new construction, were considered by SCC to be comparatively unimportant. The "bulldozer" approach of tearing down all buildings on a site was used on all the Moses projects, for this was the simplest way of assuring that slums would be destroyed. Until 1954, the federal law made the bulldozer approach almost mandatory, but Moses continued to use it after 1954 and showed nothing but hostility towards ideas of conservation and rehabilitation.

SCC paid as little attention as possible to the site residents. Where they relocated themselves was of no concern to SCC. Its philosophy of dealing with the site residents was most succinctly summed up by a leading member of the SCC staff, who stated, "Neighborhood groups are crap."

Moses could afford to ignore the site residents because he had successfully neutralized the other actors in SCC's environment. His acceptability to Democratic Party leaders, the support of the financial community and the mass media, and the forces he could muster from the various government agencies he headed assured him comparative independence from the Mayor. No mayor could afford to alienate such a powerful cluster of supporters except under very special circumstances. Since Moses cooperated with the Democratic Party leaders, he was also assured of an easy time with the Board of Estimate. SCC's program of building the maximum number of projects at high rentals pleased both the financial community and those members of the Democratic Party who obtained sponsorships or who were named as architects, appraisers, or relocaters.

If Moses need have no fear of the Mayor and the Board of Estimate, he was able to show openly his disdain for the influence of the civic groups. Moses' dislike for such organizations as CHPC, the Citizens Union, and United Neighborhood Houses extended back almost to the beginning of his career and was probably due to a facet of his vivid personality. He respected people who did things and disliked people who criticized. To him the civic organizations represented simply an assemblage of critics who were incapable of getting a road or housing project built.

Moses also managed to neutralize the other official groups that the rules of the game had placed in a position to veto his urban renewal plans. He was, himself, a member of CPC, and his personality and power were sufficient to assure that the commission would follow his lead. HHFA was also reluctant to lay obstructions in Moses' path. Moses did not hesitate to threaten to appeal to the mass media, public opinion, or the courts when the federal government got in his way.[12] It rarely did.

During the ten years of SCC's existence, it accomplished a great deal of work. As of October, 1959, sixteen projects containing over 28,000 dwelling units had been completed or were being built under the Title I program, and 314 acres had been cleared. Fourteen more projects were planned for the next three years.[13] This work was, however, achieved at the cost of much unhappiness.

Public discontent with the Title I program began to build up almost as soon as the program got underway. There were charges of favoritism and shady dealing in the choice of sponsors. Several of the sponsors chosen had had financial dealings with the Federation Bank and Trust Company while they were being considered for a project, even though Shanahan, the president of the bank, was the man who passed on the financial fitness of prospective sponsors. A number of the sponsors who were approved turned out to be financially unfit for the task of building a project. On May 22, 1952, in the midst of the City Hall contract signing for the Harlem project, it was discovered that the principals did not have the money to pay for the land. A new group was formed, which, after making the down payment on the land, had only $5,000 in working capital left. Five years later the same group had $8,891.90 available to meet $236,757.88 in unpaid bills. Manhattantown's original sponsors had $12,650 in working capital after the down payment. They eventually forfeited their sponsorship, as did the syndicate that sponsored the Pratt Institute project and the syndicate that sponsored the NYU-Bellevue project.

The Manhattantown project represented the worst of the Title I "scandals." It seems quite likely that the original syndicate that took over the land and buildings had little intention of actually constructing the project. The slums on the site produced a monthly rent roll of close to $175,000. For a period of five years the sponsors were content to leave the buildings standing, neglect maintenance, and collect the rents that came in. Other profits were made by interested parties through such means as buying all the radiators in the buildings and then selling them back to the sponsors for a higher price. Finally, in July, 1957, the original sponsors forfeited and William Zeckendorf's Webb and Knapp took over.[14]

Even after Webb and Knapp had completed the project, there was much discontent with it. This dissatisfaction was caused by factors common to most of the other Title I projects. The most significant problem was relocation. Close to 15,000 people were forced to move from the Manhattantown site to make way for the project. It was charged that many of these people moved into other slum quarters, although the law required that they be moved to "decent, safe, and sanitary" dwellings. It seems quite probable that a sizable number of the site dwellers moved to the blocks immediately surrounding the project, thus aggravating already bad slum conditions. One thing is certain: almost none of the site dwellers moved back into the new project, for the rents were considerably above what they could afford. Another aspect of relocation was the hardship it worked on the small businessmen who had been on the site. They received inadequate compensation for the condemnation of their stores, and in many cases were forced to go out of business. Other criticisms of the Title I program included the use of the bulldozer approach, the architecture and layout of the new buildings, and the fact that public resources and the power of condemnation were used to permit a private investor to make a profit.

Finally, there was discontent because of the lack of "citizen participation." The Housing Act of 1949 stated that local citizen participation in an urban renewal program was a prerequisite for federal approval. Most of the communities in the country who took advantage of the Title I program interpreted this to mean that a citywide committee of leading citizens and business leaders should be appointed to advise the local urban renewal agency. The HHFA accepted this interpretation. SCC, however, made no attempt to meet the requirements of citizen participation. New York had no citywide advisory committee, and SCC did not encourage participation on the neighborhood level. Many people in New York felt that the absence of neighborhood participation was more serious than the lack of a citywide committee. They pointed out that those people who were most directly affected by the projects, the persons living on the site, had no voice in whether or not there was to be a project and, if there was to be one, what kind of project it should be.

In 1956 James Felt was automatically given a seat on SCC

when he was appointed head of CPC. Felt had at one time been one of Moses' protégés, but a break occurred, leaving some hostility between them. Felt was disturbed by the activities of SCC, but he felt himself powerless to bring about a change. In 1958 he was joined on SCC by J. Clarence Davies, Jr., who had been appointed Director of Real Estate for the city. Felt and Davies were both real estate men by profession, and they had known each other for a long time. Their views on governmental matters were remarkably similar, and Davies shared Felt's dislike for the way the urban renewal program was being run.

Coinciding with the alliance of Davies and Felt were certain political events that were also to play a part in the future of SCC. The Democratic Party in New York City was being split by a Reform movement, which was trying to seize control of the party. For Mayor Wagner this meant that the regular party organization became less important and that a possible alternative base of support was available. (In the 1961 primary campaign for the Democratic mayoralty nomination Wagner did, in fact, break with the regulars and side with the Reformers.) Wagner and Moses disliked each other. As the regular party organization declined in strength and Wagner played with the idea of siding with the Reformers and the civic groups (both of which had been highly critical of SCC), the possibility of Moses being dropped by the Mayor grew.

In June, 1959, public indignation against the Title I program reached a climax. The agitation centered around the disclosure of the connection between certain sponsors and Shanahan's Federation Bank and Trust Company. The New York *Times*, a paper that had been a strong Moses supporter and was not noted for its muckraking, ran a lengthy series of articles reviewing the past difficulties of Title I and bringing to light some new and unfavorable information.

Moses defended Shanahan against these accusations, but Felt and Davies publicly refused to back Moses' defense. Amid demands for a thorough reform or complete abolition of the committee, the Mayor appointed three new members—Joseph Mc-Murray, John D. Butt, and Jack Straus. Butt and Straus were private citizens without governmental affiliation. McMurray, the president of Queensborough Community College, had been State Housing Commissioner and executive director of the City Housing Authority. Moses, under pressure, took away from Shanahan the task of passing on the qualifications of prospective sponsors and handed this duty over to a subcommittee consisting of Felt, Davies, and Butt. The center of power had shifted from Moses to the members of this subcommittee.

The Housing and Redevelopment Board. At the same time that Wagner appointed the three new members to SCC, he also took steps to appease those who desired more drastic changes by appointing J. Anthony Panuch as his special adviser on Housing and Urban Renewal. Panuch, a former associate of Governor Dewey and an experienced former federal official, set about making a study of the city's housing programs with a view to suggesting basic changes. In March, 1960, Panuch issued his final report on the administration of the urban renewal program.[15] He recommended that the Title I program and all other housing programs except public housing be placed under the jurisdiction of a three-man Housing and Redevelopment Board that would have the status of a regular city department and be equipped with a sizable staff of its own.

The anomalous position of Moses, heading a committee he no longer controlled, and the strong public sentiment in favor of a change led to the resignation of Moses from SCC and the implementation of the Panuch proposals. Moses, in resigning, declared that the Title I program was "a dead duck."

In May, 1960, the State legislature gave final approval to the creation of the Housing and Redevelopment Board (HRB). Wagner appointed Davies as chairman. Robert Weaver, who had been State Rent Administrator under Governor Harriman and was chairman of the board of NAACP, and Walter Fried, who resigned his post as administrator of Region One for HHFA, were appointed as the other two members of HRB.

Davies had entered city service to undertake the job of cleaning up the corruption-ridden Bureau of Real Estate. He reorganized the Bureau, won it the status of a regular city department, and became the first Commissioner of Real Estate. He viewed his role as chairman of HRB as in some respects similar to the job he had performed as head of the Real Estate Bureau. He wanted to clear the name of the urban renewal program in the same way that he had reformed the city's real estate affairs. Thus, he put great emphasis on making sure that all potential sponsors were financially qualified and responsible businessmen. He did not want to have any dealings with political party leaders.

Davies had been a real estate man all his life, however, and he did not share the objections that had been raised against the high rents in the Moses projects. He believed that land should be developed to its highest economic potential and that therefore the city should not subsidize rents in locations where it was not absolutely necessary to do so. He agreed with Moses that Title I projects should add to city revenues by increasing the value of the land sufficiently to pay back more in taxes than the cost of the original land subsidy.

Prior to his appointment as Director of Real Estate, Davies had had no political experience. He had been active in many civic groups, having served as president of CHPC and as treasurer of the Citizens Union. These groups had been highly critical of SCC, and Davies agreed with most of their criticisms. He shared the view of the civic groups that the needs of the site residents should be given more attention, and when he assumed the chairmanship of HRB, he made great efforts to see that all site tenants were relocated into "decent, safe, and sanitary dwellings" as the law required. In his previous post as city Real Estate Commissioner, he had been in charge of all city relocation

work, and thus had an added interest in this aspect of the
Title I program.

Davies took office with the backing of two sets of groups—
the more liberal real estate men and the civic organizations with
which Moses had fought—and two officials: CPC chairman
James Felt and Mayor Wagner. The liberal real estate men were
not so powerful as the financial community that had backed
Moses. The civic groups were vociferous, but they carried little
weight with Party leaders. Davies considered himself to be
working for the Mayor and thus duty-bound to carry out the
Mayor's directives.

Under these circumstances, Davies and the program were
quite vulnerable to attack. The road lay open for interest groups
and politicians to work through the Mayor or the Board of Estimate to block or alter any particular project. Davies had little
political ammunition with which to fight back. He was further
handicapped by the bad reputation the urban renewal program
had acquired. No matter how strongly Davies protested, in the
public mind urban renewal was still identified with Moses and
the bulldozer approach.

Davies' personal closeness to Felt and the similarity of outlook
that the two men shared made it most unlikely that HRB would
encounter opposition from CPC. HRB's relations with the federal government were eased by the fact that the other two members of the original board (Fried and Weaver) both had close
connections in Washington. Fried had been administrator of
Region One for HHFA. Weaver later resigned from the HRB
to become national administrator of HHFA.

The first major action of HRB was to issue a policy statement,
including a detailed list of the Moses-planned projects that were
being dropped, postponed, or carried out. HRB promised that
no projects would be added to the list without first having CPC
delineate the areas and that after the first year all projects would
emanate from a priority list that CPC would establish. It an-

nounced that it would advertise for sponsors for all new projects and that it would carefully investigate the qualifications of all potential sponsors. It promised to listen to the complaints or suggestions of neighborhood groups.

In February, 1961, the Mayor announced that studies would be undertaken for the first two new Title I projects that HRB had proposed. The areas to be studied were a three-block section in the Lower East Side and a sixteen-block section in the western part of Greenwich Village. The explosion that followed the announcement marked a turning point in the urban renewal program. It has often been remarked that revolutions occur not when conditions are at their worst but when they are improving. This seemed to be the case with Title I. The people on the Greenwich Village site rapidly mobilized for a full-scale battle against the study of their area. The details of this battle will be examined in Chapter IV.

For seven months HRB was preoccupied with combatting its opponents in Greenwich Village and defending itself against those whom the Villagers enlisted as allies. The stand of the Villagers emboldened other opponents of the urban renewal program. The residents of Brooklyn Heights, the residents of the Cobble Hill section of Brooklyn, and the Puerto Ricans in the West Side Urban Renewal Area (WSURA) all attacked HRB and allied themselves with the Villagers. Davies and his ally Felt were fighting for the life of their whole program. In September, 1961, on the eve of the Democratic primary election, the Mayor announced that he would ask HRB to abandon the West Village study. Davies complied.

No further Title I projects were proposed for the next two years. Work continued on WSURA and on some of the projects that had been initiated under Moses. New emphasis was placed on middle-income projects constructed under the provisions of the Mitchell-Lama Law.

In January, 1962, Davies announced his resignation. Milton

Mollen, who had been Davies' counsel, was named as the new HRB chairman. Mollen made one basic change in the policies of HRB. He announced that it would not propose any more "luxury" (that is, fully tax-paying) projects. Two Title I projects that had originated with Moses were in an advanced stage of planning when Mollen took office. One of these he altered to suit the wishes of the site residents, and the other he dropped completely.[16]

Although SCC and HRB are the agencies that have been primarily responsible for urban renewal in New York, a number of other governmental agencies have also played significant roles in the renewal process. Of these agencies, one of the most important has been CPC.

The City Planning Commission. CPC consisted, before 1961, of seven members—the chief engineer of the Board of Estimate, who served ex officio, and six commissioners appointed by the Mayor for overlapping terms of eight years. The Mayor appointed one of the commissioners to serve as chairman of CPC. Although appointed by the Mayor, the commissioners could not be removed except for misconduct or negligence and thus were far more independent of the Mayor than the heads of the regular city departments. The 1961 City Charter permitted the Mayor to remove the CPC chairman at his pleasure and substituted another regular commissioner for the Board of Estimate engineer.

Under the 1938 City Charter, CPC had been given great powers. It was authorized to prepare and maintain a comprehensive master plan for the city, to prepare zoning regulations, and to draw up the annual capital budget. It did not, however, have the political support necessary to exercise such broad power. A comprehensive master plan still does not exist. Not until 1961 could enough support be mustered to put through a new zoning law, and so many compromises were necessary to obtain passage of this law that it remains to be seen how effective it will be.[17]

The capital budget has each year been changed in many important respects by the Board of Estimate.

In January, 1956, Mayor Wagner appointed James Felt, a real estate man, as chairman of CPC. Felt, a shrewd political bargainer and a good administrator, gave new life to the Commission. He was aided by Mayor Wagner, who had himself been chairman of CPC for two years. The Department of City Planning, CPC's operating arm, obtained additional personnel of a high caliber and was given increased financial support. Felt became one of Wagner's most intimate advisers.

Under Felt the commission was also solidified internally. The added strength of the Department of City Planning strengthened the chairman's hand. He was the only member of CPC who had daily contact with and access to the expertise of the department, and this greatly increased his authority within the Commission. CPC was also solidified when Moses, the one commissioner whose power more than equaled Felt's, left CPC at the expiration of his term in December, 1961.

Despite this increased strength, CPC still suffered from a lack of support. Sayre and Kaufman describe its constituency as "unstable, largely unstructured, and containing at any one moment many more voices of criticism and dissent than dependable sources of support." [18] In the field of urban renewal CPC could depend only on the support of some of the civic groups. Its independence, established by the rules and also by the myths surrounding the sanctity of planning and planners, made it less vulnerable to influence by the Mayor or the Board of Estimate but at the same time made it less able to draw on support from either of these sources. The Board of Estimate retained and freely exercised the power to change many of the commission's decisions.[19]

In 1958, when the Urban Renewal Board was established to administer the plan for WSURA, the Department of City Planning became an operating agency in the field of urban renewal.

This role was greatly increased after 1960, when Davies became head of HRB. The cooperation of Davies and Felt brought the Department of City Planning into the process of selecting urban renewal sites and determining the nature of proposed projects. The division of functions between HRB and City Planning was often quite fluid. Sometimes one agency would select a site, sometimes the other, but throughout the process there was the closest possible cooperation between HRB and the City Planning Department.

The Mayor and the Board of Estimate. Robert Wagner was elected Mayor in November, 1953, and reelected in 1957 with the backing of the regular Democratic Party organization. Sayre and Kaufman have pointed out, however, that Wagner's administration was "characterized much less by Tammany dominance than by Wagner's independence." [20] This independence increased, so that in 1961 Wagner decided to side with the Reform faction of the Party and to base his primary campaign on opposition to "bossism" and the regulars. The campaign was successful, although Wagner's victory must be attributed to many factors in addition to the support of the Reformers.

Wagner's independence from Party leaders has in part been due to the weakness of the regular Party organization. While New York remains essentially a one-party Democratic city, the weakening of the Party, begun in the 1930s, has been greatest and most apparent since the rise of the Reform movement in the mid-1950s. In recent years the Mayor has had to search for support wherever he can get it and thus has been open to the appeals of labor unions, civic groups, and many other claimants. The backing of the Reformers often cannot be depended upon, for the rank and file of the Reform clubs have been generally hostile to Wagner, and their leaders have not hesitated to oppose him on many issues.

The lack of strong Party organization has also reduced the ability of the Mayor to defend his official family. Since he must seek support where he can find it rather than depending on a stable balance of strength from the organization, his defense of various city departments is conditioned by the political support they can provide. HRB and CPC could offer little in the way of such support. Although any political chief executive must take into account the political backing his executive agencies have, the less stable the executive's other support, the more important this factor becomes.

The Board of Estimate occupied the center of gravity in the city's political process, at least until the new City Charter was passed in 1961. It consisted of eight members—the five Borough Presidents, each of whom have two votes, and the Mayor, the President of the City Council and the Comptroller, each of whom have four votes. The Board had all the powers enjoyed by most city legislatures. For all practical purposes it controlled both the finances and the personnel of the city government.[21]

The weekly meetings of the Board are open to the public, and any individual or representative of an organization who wants to speak is permitted to do so. All decisions of the Board, however, are arrived at in the executive sessions, which it holds prior to the public meetings. The Board members almost never debate issues among themselves during public sessions.

The Borough Presidents usually have close ties to the leaders of the Democratic Party organization. In New York the boundaries of the five counties are the same as the boundaries of the five boroughs, and the County Leader is the key figure in the Party organization. Since the Borough Presidents are elected by the voters of their particular borough, they are quite sensitive to the needs and wishes of their County Leader.

The Borough Presidents also provide a convenient channel for noncitywide interest groups to influence city policy. Because the City Council lacks any effective power, the Borough Presidents are the only important policy-makers whose constituency is lo-

calized. Their usefulness in serving as spokesmen for neighborhood interests is enhanced by the Board of Estimate's equivalent
of senatorial courtesy. By custom, if a Borough President ob-
jects to any proposal that affects only his own borough, the
other Borough Presidents will not vote in favor of that proposal.

In matters concerning physical changes in an area, the Borough President of Manhattan has institutionalized his concern
for neighborhood feeling by setting up twelve local planning
boards. The members of the local planning boards are chosen by
the Borough President, and each of the boards reports its recommendations to the Borough President. Since 1951, when then-
Borough President Wagner established the boards, their influence has varied widely, depending on the Borough President and
the composition of the particular board.[22] The new City Charter of 1961 provides for local planning boards to be set up in all
five boroughs.[23]

The factionalism within the Democratic Party has influenced
the Borough Presidents as well as the Mayor and has probably
made them more attentive to the interest groups within their respective boroughs. Whether a problem is brought to his attention by a district leader or by an interest group, the Borough
President remains the official most likely to be sensitive to the
discontent of a neighborhood.

The Housing and Home Finance Agency. HHFA was established in 1947 to provide a single agency that would be responsible for the principal federal housing programs and functions. It
consists of the office of the administrator, two constituent units
—the Community Facilities Administration and the Urban Renewal Adminisration—and three constituent agencies—the
Federal Housing Administration (FHA), the Public Housing
Administration, and the Federal National Mortgage Association.[24] HHFA has seven regional offices. Region One covers
New York and the New England states.

The Urban Renewal Administration is responsible for carry-

ing out the Title I program and most other aspects of urban renewal. It requires the local government to submit what is known
as a "workable program" before undertaking any renewal project. The workable program consists of seven requirements that
the community must meet. The local government must prove
that it has an adequate system of housing codes and ordinances,
an effective administrative organization for implementing urban
renewal, a factual analysis of the conditions of its neighborhoods
as a basis for determining the treatment required, a comprehensive plan (either completed or in preparation) for the development of the city, a capacity to meet the financial obligations and
requirements of the program, adequate organization and plans
for rehousing people displaced by government action including
urban renewal, and evidence that the program has been prepared
with citizen participation and that it has citizen support.[25] The
requirements of the workable program have not been rigidly enforced, and in its early days the program came to be called the
"seven promises." [26] Some of the requirements, such as the one
calling for a comprehensive development plan, could probably
be met by only a very few, if any, of the major cities in the
country. Other requirements, such as having an adequate relocation plan, are very difficult for HHFA to check because they
require information that can be obtained only by investing great
financial and manpower resources. HHFA is thus often forced
to accept the figures provided by the local community.

Although the workable program is not strictly enforced,
HHFA does carefully scrutinize all plans for urban renewal
projects and often raises questions or suggests changes to the
local agency. The examination of renewal plans is usually carried out by the regional offices of HHFA. Urban renewal plans
submitted by large cities like New York are usually subject to
extensive negotiation and discussion between the local agency
and the office of the HHFA regional administrator.

Such negotiation has often delayed the approval and execution of projects in New York. HHFA has, however, never exercised its power to veto flatly a renewal project in New York, although it has occasionally threatened to do so.[27] It is reluctant to intervene in local controversies, and complaints or inquiries from private persons or groups are generally passed on to the local agency without comment.

These five governmental groups—HRB, CPC, the Mayor, the Board of Estimate, and HHFA—are each in a position to veto any renewal proposal. In New York at present, no extragovernmental mechanism, such as a political party, can unify these different groups and assure action on some particular issue. Moses managed to construct a "public works political machine" which helped to assure action, but after his downfall the urban renewal system became as loosely integrated as the overall political structure of the city.[28] Nongovernmental groups were presented with a variety of access points, each of which provided sufficient leverage to stop the city from taking action.

The three case studies that follow span the entire period between the early years of Moses and the early years of Milton Mollen. Each of the cases reflects the influence of the city's changing political structure, the kinds of groups that will be active in renewal controversies, and the uses that these groups make of the available access points.

CHAPTER III

Seaside-Hammels

On the southern side of Long Island, facing out on the Atlantic, there is a thin strip of flat sandy land known as the Rockaway Peninsula (Figure 1). The Peninsula is about 11 miles long and is separated from Long Island by Jamaica Bay on the north. The communities on the Peninsula, which are known collectively as the Rockaways, are formally a part of the Borough of Queens, which in turn is one of the five boroughs constituting New York City.

The Peninsula is comparatively isolated from the rest of New York. The city subway has a spur line which runs to the Rockaways, but it is a double-fare trip to the center of the city, and it takes about an hour to reach midtown Manhattan from the nearest point in the Rockaways. Travel by car is not much faster. This isolation has had a noticeable effect upon the inhabitants of the Peninsula. A report on the Rockaways by the Community Renewal Section of the New York City Planning Commission noted that, "In no previous report has there been as much feeling of a 'city' within but apart from the city." [1] A multiplicity of local groups has been one manifestation of this feeling.

This sense of apartness has existed in various forms throughout the history of the Rockaways. Around the turn of the century the peninsula was an upper-class summer resort to which society leaders retreated from the heat of Manhattan.

In the 1920s and 1930s many city dwellers discovered the

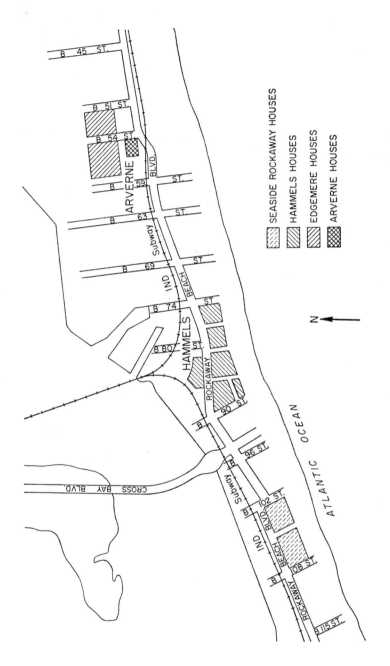

FIGURE I. THE ROCKAWAY PENINSULA

Rockaways. Improved transportation facilities made it possible for thousands of New Yorkers to rent a small bungalow for the summer and enjoy the fine beaches on the Atlantic. At the same time, the year-round residential population grew. Most of the permanent settlers were upper middle-class Jews, although Irish and Italian communities were also established. The geography of the peninsula facilitated the separation of the settlers on ethnic and economic lines, so that each of the subcommunities tended to take on an identifiable character that distinguished it from the neighboring areas. This separation has been maintained, and today it is possible to distinguish fourteen such subcommunities along the 11-mile strip of land. The distinctiveness of each of these areas is such that their boundaries are "universally accepted" by the inhabitants and are "disputed only within a block or two." [2] The economic character of these areas runs the gamut from the high-income luxury houses of the Neponsit section to the wretched slum dwellings in Hammels and Arverne.

During the 1950s the population of the Rockaways changed greatly. The number of permanent residents increased from 51,103 in 1950 to 64,314 in 1957. The population of the Peninsula is still growing at a rapid pace, and estimates of the number of year-round inhabitants in 1962 ranged from 75,000 to 94,000. [3] Most of this increase was due to the large amount of residential construction that took place and to the improvement of transportation lines to Manhattan.

The number of people who rent houses for the summer is still considerable. The Chamber of Commerce estimated in 1962 that there were about 50,000 summer residents. Since World War II, however, there has been a steady decline in the summer population. There is every indication that the trend away from seasonal rentals in the Rockaways will continue. The area is adjusting to becoming less a summer resort and more a year-round community. This adjustment entails great changes in the economic basis of the residents.

The most significant change that has occurred, however, the change that has "split the peninsula with fear and tension," [4] is the influx of a significant number of Negroes into the community. The first Negroes came to the Rockaways in the 1920s and 1930s as domestic help for some of the wealthier families. At the end of World War II there were two small Negro settlements —one in Redfern and the other in Hammels. Starting in the late 1940s and continuing into the 1950s, the Negro population of Hammels was swelled by "multiproblem families" who were assigned to housing there by the City's Department of Welfare. The Department was faced with the problem of finding low-rent housing for narcotics addicts, alcoholics, unwed mothers, and other individuals who were not eligible for public housing. It was discovered that the old wooden bungalows in Hammels, which had originally been built for the summertime use of vacationers, were suitable places to house such people. Aside from being cheap and available, the bungalows also had the advantage of moving the problem families to a place where they would not cause too much trouble and where they would not be too noticeable. The completion of three public housing projects— Arverne Houses in 1951, Redfern Houses in 1953, and Hammels Houses in 1955—also added to the Negro population. Negroes moved into these projects, and those Negroes who had been living on the sites gravitated to the Hammels area.

This influx of Negroes into the Rockaways caused much anguish and hostility among the white residents. To the Chamber of Commerce and the civic associations, the Negroes represented a threat to property values. For the Chamber of Commerce, they also represented a threat to the picture it hoped to create of a prosperous, year-round, middle-income community. For many of the residents, both summer and year-round, the Negroes were probably a symbol of the central city from which they were trying to escape.

The hostility toward the Negroes took several forms. It became impossible for a Negro to move into any of the predominantly white areas. Negroes found that many employers in the area refused to hire them. The residents also took steps to prevent any further increase in the Negro population. Violent opposition developed toward any additional public housing projects. Edgemere Houses, which had been planned as a low-income project to absorb the site tenants from the Title I projects, was changed in 1959 to a middle-income project because of community pressure. The whole history of the Seaside-Hammels Title I projects is inseparable from the background of the white community's hostility to the Negroes.

It is clearly a distortion to talk about the Rockaway community as if it were a homogeneous entity with a single viewpoint. The isolation of the community and its heterogeneity lead to the formation of many groups. Changes in the leadership of these groups are frequent, and alliances tend to shift according to the issue. But all the groups must compete for the attention of the central city—for space to present their views in central-city newspapers, for services from city departments, and for favors and assistance from citywide private groups. This situation leads to the kaleidoscopic pattern of groups and alliances characteristic of the Rockaways.

It is possible, however, to identify the factions and alliances that form around any issue. For the purposes of this case study, one can discern four elements in the community that played a major part in the urban renewal controversy: (1) the Chamber of Commerce, (2) the civic associations, (3) the "liberal community," and (4) the "Negro community."

The Chamber of Commerce is the dominant organization in the Rockaways. Its membership consists of all the large real estate holders and the vast majority of the business community. One informant estimated that 85–90 percent of all private real estate on the Peninsula was held in whole or in part by members of the Chamber. The Chamber is the only organization in the community that employs a full-time professional staff.

Almost all the subcommunities on the Rockaways are represented by their own civic association. In 1962 an investigator for CPC counted fifteen such organizations.[5] The civic associations usually consist of homeowners in the area, although some of them also include the local small businessmen. A peak association —the Rockaway Council of Civic Organizations—attempts to coordinate the efforts of the various neighborhood associations, but it does not speak for the civic associations as a whole.[6]

Most of the civic associations are subject to rapid changes in leadership and organization. Some are groups that consist basically of one member who has the time and motivation to issue press releases. If he loses interest or moves elsewhere, the group disintegrates. Other civic associations are more broadly based, but almost all are maintained and controlled by a small handful of people, with the nominal members not taking any interest in, and not being very aware of, what the leadership does. The leaders usually do not have much stature in the community and may easily be ousted and replaced by another small group of leaders.

A more or less permanent rift exists between the Chamber of Commerce and the civic associations. The main cause of this rift is the fact that they represent different interests in the community. The civic associations have tended to fight any major expansion or change in the area and have been somewhat hostile to the transient summer residents. The Chamber has tried to promote increased population, both permanent and summer, because such increases are good for real estate and other business. Another issue that has divided the civic associations and the Chamber is the fare to be charged on the subway line to the Rockaways. The present fare is 30 cents. The civic associations, many of whose members commute to work, have pressed for a lower rate. The Chamber of Commerce originally wanted a 40-

cent fare and has now become a defender of the existing 30-cent fare. It fears that a lower fare will encourage people to travel to Manhattan or to Nassau County (where there is no city sales tax) to do their shopping.

This basic difference of interest has been reinforced by, and is reflected in, an accumulation of grievances and epithets. The Chamber of Commerce is very much aware that it has a staff and does things in a professional, businesslike way. It considers the civic associations "a bunch of amateurs." Also, the Chamber considers itself the only truly representative organization in the community. The other associations are "newcomers," "one-man outfits," "two-dollar organizations," or a bunch of "civicticians." On the other hand, the civic associations tend to believe that all the decisions of the Chamber are based on motives of private gain and that the civic associations are the only groups that consider the public welfare.

The split between the Chamber and the civic associations does not, however, prevent them from sometimes working together. The Chamber's staff will often alert the civic associations to some event or proposal that affects the community. On certain issues the Chamber will try to get some of the civic associations to join it in taking action. The Chamber, however, is jealous of its right to speak for the community. In 1954, when a meeting was held to form a joint civic council, the Chamber said it would sit in on the meetings and would even provide money for a secretary, but it wanted the council to refrain from issuing publicity and from binding its members to decisions.

The split between the Chamber and the civic associations is not so great as the division between the Chamber and the civic associations, on the one hand, and the liberals and Negroes on the other. The "liberals" may loosely be defined as that segment of the white community that sympathizes with the plight of the Negroes in the Rockaways. The most active liberal organization has been the Rockaway Council for Relocation and Slum Prevention. The Relocation Council was formed by the Rockaway Health Council in 1959 as an *ad hoc* organization to deal with the problems of relocation from the Title I sites. The driving force behind the Relocation Council has been Helen Rausnitz, although she shares the chairmanship with the Reverend Joseph May, a Negro minister in the Arverne area. Mrs. Rausnitz, a housewife with three children, began her organizational activities in P-TA work and gradually became interested in other problems facing the community.

The Relocation Council represents a coalition of two groupings on the peninsula—the liberal Jews and the middle-class Negroes. The Jews are represented specifically by the American Jewish Committee and also provide the leadership for some of the P-TA's. The basis for the alliance seems to be primarily ideological, at least on the part of the Jews, who are motivated by a desire to cope with a major community problem. The middle-class Negroes are penalized socially and economically by the failure of the rest of the community to distinguish among the different segments of the Negro population, and thus they have a stake in trying to raise the status and improve the condition of all Negroes on the peninsula.

The Negro community in the Hammels-Arverne area is sharply divided, primarily on the basis of economic class. The middle-class Negroes live mostly in the public housing projects. They attend the Reverend Mr. May's Mt. Carmel Baptist Church, and they provide most of the small membership of the local NAACP and Urban League. About 10 to 20 percent of the Negroes in Arverne-Hammels would probably fall into the middle-class category. As the Reverend Mr. May's association with Mrs. Rausnitz indicates, the middle-class Negroes and the liberal whites are closely allied.

The remainder of the Negro community consists of people who are poor, who live in squalid conditions, and who are generally cut off from the world outside. The leadership of this lower-class segment of the community is concentrated in one person—Leonard Scarbrough.

Scarbrough first came to the Rockaways in 1926, when he was seventeen years old, as a domestic working for a wealthy Jewish family. After World War II he began his organizational activities. He succeeded in using his forceful personality to pyramid economic and political gains, until today he has a monopoly of leadership. He has been president of the only Negro political club, the Arverne-Hammels Democratic Association (formerly the Colored Democrat Association), since 1947. He has acquired large real estate holdings of his own and acts as agent for the real estate men who have holdings in Hammels (supposedly including the local Assemblyman, J. Lewis Fox). He is the primary money-lender for the Negro community. This position gives him leverage over other businesses because he often suggests where borrowers should spend their money. He is highly influential in the affairs of the large local Negro church, St. John Baptist, and there is good reason to believe that he exercises as much, if not more, influence than the minister in the affairs of the church. The situation in Hammels suggests the possibility that in some cases the Negro churches may be a means used by those who have economic and political power and that the independent influence of religion and the clergy in Negro life has been exaggerated.

Scarbrough is disowned by the middle-class members of the Negro community. Both they and the liberals mistrust his ends and dislike his tactics. They believe that he is out only for personal gain and point to the fact that the buildings he owns are among the most rundown in the area.

The division in the Negro community is quite sharp. For example, no members of the Reverend Mr. May's church are members of Scarbrough's political club. Thus, the Negro leadership best able to deal with the white community is cut off from the bulk of the Negro population.

We have now briefly described the major local forces in the Rockaways that played a part in the urban renewal controversy. The other groups on the Peninsula did not play a large role. The local Republican Club took no position in relation to the projects. The local Democratic club was controlled by Frank Crisona, the Queens Borough President. Crisona, as we shall see later, was interested in the projects, but his aims were best implemented by use of his position as Borough President rather than through his club. The local newspaper, *The Wave*, tended to side editorially with the Chamber of Commerce, perhaps because its advertising revenue was derived largely from the Chamber members. The paper printed articles submitted by all groups in the community, however, and its editorial opinions do not seem to have had much influence on its news columns.

We shall now turn to the specific events that occurred in connection with the urban renewal projects. This will enable us to see the community groups in action.

SEASIDE AND HAMMELS PROJECTS

Location and Nature of the Projects, 1953–54. On May 22, 1953, Moses sent a brief memo to his chief assistant, William Lebwohl. The memo was attached to a newspaper clipping about the Rockaways. "What would you think of a Title One project at Rockaway?" he queried. "The writedown would be very small." Two days later Lebwohl replied favorably to the suggestion, and the search for funds and sponsors for the project began.[7]

This was not the first time that Moses had thought about putting a housing project in the Rockaways. His first major public announcement concerning housing, a booklet put out in 1938, contained detailed plans for a project to be built from Beach-73rd Street to Beach-94th Street in the Rockaways. The plans called for a limited-dividend project of 20,000 rooms to be built by private developers.[8] For various reasons this proposal was dropped, but few ideas ever drop completely from Moses' head. In the back of his mind remained the idea of a housing project for the Rockaways, perhaps to supplement the other public improvements he had brought to the Peninsula.

The idea was also not a new one to some of the leading citizens of the Rockaways. In 1951 George Wolpert, the Executive Director of the Rockaways Chamber of Commerce, had corresponded with his friend Thomas Shanahan, a member of the Mayor's Committee on Slum Clearance and an intimate of Moses, about the idea of a Title I project for the Rockaways. In September, 1953, when Wolpert found out that such a project was again under consideration, he wrote to Moses, enclosing his previous correspondence with Shanahan and expressing enthusiasm about the project. Moses replied, "If we can work it out, I would be inclined to recommend such a project for the Rockaways. . . . We may have to look to some organization for support on this. If we need it, I shall call you." [9]

By November, Moses had been assured that federal money was available for the project. By the beginning of December he had obtained a commitment from a sponsor, and he notified Lebwohl, "O.K.—Let's notify the committee and go ahead." [10] The "committee" was SCC, officially responsible for the execution of the Title I program.

On December 13, Moses announced to the public that a study would be made of the Rockaways for a Title I project.[11] The Rockaway community was not slow to react to the announcement.

The first public reaction came from the Negro community in Hammels. The Arverne-Hammels Democratic Club, which was dominated by Scarbrough, met and declared that they were opposed to any clearance whatsoever. It was natural that the residents of the Negro community would react as they did, for they had been subject to much hostility from other Rockaway groups and their position on the Peninsula was not secure. Furthermore, they were familiar with the personal consequences of public projects, many of them having been forced to move from the sites of the Redfern public housing project and the Hammels public housing project. Scarbrough was especially sensitive to the possible effects of a project, not only because his political leadership was based on the existing Negro community but also because he had a large economic stake in the continuance of the community as it existed.

The location of the proposed project soon became a major issue. By February it became public knowledge that Moses was considering the Beach-103rd–Beach-108th area of Seaside. This site was chosen at the request of the sponsor, Joel Schenker of the HRH Construction Company. Schenker, like all renewal sponsors, was primarily interested not in clearing slums but in making a profit on his investment. The better the area in which the project was located, the higher the rents that could be charged by the sponsor and the better his chances of renting. Also, the Seaside site presented far fewer problems of relocation than did the Hammels site. The sponsor would tend to pick the best possible area that could still be justified as a slum to meet the requirements of the Title I law.

The interests of the sponsor did not coincide with the interests of most of the Rockaway community. They wanted to get rid of the slums, specifically the slums that constituted the Negro community in Hammels. The February issue of the *Rockaway Review*, the official publication of the Chamber of Commerce, stated that the selection of the Seaside site had come as a surprise, and that the Chamber had recommended a study in the area between Beach-73rd Street and Beach-95th Street in Hammels.

Two other groups were especially vocal in objecting to the selection of the Seaside site. The owners of property in Seaside, represented by the Seaside Property Owners Association, objected that the area was not a slum and should not be taken by the city. One owner of thirty-four bungalows on the site wrote to Moses asking, "How in God's name can you contemplate *taking* my property, which is in excellent condition and transfer it over to another private party to build and rent and put me out of business? This is my livelihood. Is this constitutional and the American way?" [12]

The owners of property in Hammels, represented by the Rockaway Beach Property Owners and Civic Association, also objected, but they were unhappy because their property was not being taken. In the past few years, conditions had forced them to rent to Negroes, whom they considered undesirable tenants. They felt that their property had fallen in value and that the neighborhood was no longer a pleasant place to live. In short, they wanted to get out, and condemnation by the city seemed an ideal way to accomplish their objective. For a while, the Seaside and Rockaway Beach organizations cooperated in their efforts to have the site of the project changed.

Thomas A. Caligiuri, the president of the Somerville-Arverne Civic Association, wrote to Moses saying that he understood that Moses had originally considered the Beach-73rd Street–Beach-95th Street site and then had switched to Beach-103rd Street to Beach-108th. The Association, said Caligiuri, wanted to go on record as favoring the original site.[13] Moses replied, "I do not recall that we ever had a plan that started at B73 Street and went to B95 Street." [14]

The Caligiuri letter and the objections of other groups did, however, have an effect. Moses started considering a second Rockaway project,[15] and an inspector was sent out to the Hammels site.[16] The miserable conditions that existed there were reported, and on March 3, William Spargo, one of Moses' chief assistants, wrote to the Somerville-Arverne Civic Association that the Beach-73rd Street area "is in our immediate plans for redevelopment" and that they would "concentrate upon it as soon as the Seaside area is settled." [17]

By this time community opposition to the Seaside site had reached a high pitch. The Rockaway Beach Businessmen's Association called a mass protest meeting "to locate proposed Rockaway Beach housing where it is urgently needed. Namely B73 to B83 Streets." The call for the meeting was supported by the Somerville-Arverne Civic Association, the Rockaway Beach Property Owners' Association, and three other civic associations on the Peninsula.

Shortly after the protest meeting, Wolpert added the voice of the Chamber of Commerce to the community pressure by writing Moses that, "The entire community is anxious to have the area between B74 and B83 Streets, from Rockaway Beach Boulevard to the oceanfront cleaned up. . . . The Rockaways can never be properly developed unless we can get rid of this slum and welfare condition." [18] Moses' reply was more definite than Spargo's letter of three weeks before:

The City's coordinated program for slum clearance and housing includes redevelopment of the area between B73 and B86 Streets. When the plans for such redevelopment have been more fully formulated, they will be publicized and I am sure will meet with the approval of all civic interests in the community.[19]

Towards the end of April, *The Wave* published a story that stated that SCC planned to build a Title I project at Seaside and make it part Title I and part low-cost and also planned to have the Housing Authority extend the low-cost Hammels public housing project.[20] On May 11 Philip Cruise, chairman of the New York City Housing Authority, Moses, and Herman Stichman, Chairman of the State Housing Authority, issued a joint statement proposing a state housing project and a tax-paying project for the Seaside and Hammels sites and other low-rental project in the Mott Basin area.

Wolpert was quite disturbed when he read of this document in the *Long Island Daily Press*. For one thing, he had not been consulted about the projects or notified in advance. Moses, Stich-

man, and Cruise had visited the Hammels site, and Wolpert had
not been invited to come along. Secondly, the Chamber of Commerce was strongly opposed to putting a low-rent project in the
Mott Basin area. "This is an area where many high-type homes
are located and is one of the finest residential areas in our community," wrote Wolpert.[21] (Cruise told Lebwohl, Moses' right-
hand man, that there was some truth in Wolpert's comments
about the Mott Basin area.[22]) Thirdly, Wolpert was still unhappy about putting a project in Seaside. The Chamber had almost 100 members located on the site.

The Chamber also objected to making part of the Hammels
site low-cost. It was opposed on this point by the Rockaway
Beach Businessmen's Association, which stated that it would be
"discriminating against the working class" if low-cost housing
were barred from the Rockaways.

Meanwhile, Scarbrough continued to be uneasy about the fate
of the Negro community. In April the Arverne-Hammels Democratic Association started a "Clean-up, Paint-up, Fix-up" campaign.[23] On May 3 the Association held a mass meeting to discuss public housing for the Rockaways.[24] Scarbrough wrote
Mayor Wagner that the Hammels area was not a slum and that
Negroes were being refused accommodations in some housing
projects.[25]

It was the Chamber of Commerce that finally proved trium-
phant. Cruise chose the occasion of the Chamber's annual dinner
to announce that the Hammels site would be all Title I and that
the low-cost project would not be located in the Mott Basin area
but in the area between Somerville and Conch Basins.[26] (This
did not please the people of Somerville. Caligiuri, speaking for
the Somerville-Arverne Civic Association, stated that they
would "do everything possible to oppose low-cost housing in
the Somerville-Arverne area." [27]) Said Wolpert, "The plan co-
incides with the wishes of the Chamber and gives the organiza-

tion all it had requested." [28] This was not strictly true, since the Chamber was still unhappy about the Seaside project. It had come to the conclusion, however, that this price was worth paying for the clearance of Hammels and for the general improvement of the community that would result from two large high-rental projects.

On November 18, 1954, about a year and a half after the project had first been considered, SCC published a booklet containing detailed plans for the Seaside project. The plans for Hammels were still in a preliminary stage.

From Planning to Demolition, 1954–60. By the end of 1954, the fact that there would be two projects, one located in Seaside and the other in Hammels, was clearly established and was accepted by most of the Rockaway community. Five years was to pass, however, before the sponsor of the project actually acquired title to the sites. Actual demolition for the projects did not begin until 1960. Between the end of 1954 and the beginning of demolition, a number of controversies arose concerning the projects. The major debate concerned when the condemnation of the sites would take place. Some groups were interested in having condemnation take place as soon as possible, while others wanted to delay the process. In addition to this debate, there were a number of other issues that aroused certain elements of the community. We shall deal with two such issues—the relocation of St. John Baptist Church, and the controversy over the height of the project buildings. We turn first to the issue of when condemnation would take place.

In January, 1955, Wolpert wrote to Moses suggesting that condemnation of property on the Seaside site be delayed till after the summer, thus allowing owners to rent their cottages for another season. Wolpert also urged that planning for the Hammels project be speeded up. Moses, who may have thought the Chamber had already gotten enough, reacted negatively to Wolpert's letter. He passed it on to his assistant, Spargo, with a note stating, "I don't like this letter at all. I think we should clamp down on Wolpert." [29]

The question of summer rentals was an important one for the community. About 450 bungalows and 18 large rooming houses in Seaside and 250–300 dwelling units—mostly in rooming houses–in Hammels were involved. The Chamber of Commerce estimated that total income from summer rentals in the two areas came to about $500,000 a year.[30] The Seaside site accounted for the major part of this income, and most of the bungalow owners on the site were members of the Chamber. Thus, the Chamber was primarily concerned with continuing summer rentals in Seaside. The Chamber and the white property owners wanted demolition of Hammels to begin as soon as possible.

Actually in 1955 the decision as to when to condemn the property in the two areas did not hinge on the Chamber of Commerce or on Moses' opinion of Wolpert. Sometime late in 1954 or early in 1955, Schenker, the proposed sponsor of the Seaside project, decided to abandon the undertaking. In February, 1955, Moses requested planning funds for the Hammels project but was turned down by the Board of Estimate because of a dispute going on between Mayor Wagner and FHA. On April 21, however, the Board of Estimate approved the planning funds for Hammels. Toward the end of July, the federal government allocated the funds for Hammels, and Moses announced that Seaside would be reactivated and a joint sponsor found for both projects. The search for a sponsor dragged on. The summer of 1956 passed with still no word as to when or whether the projects would be built. In November, 1956, however, a booklet containing detailed plans of the Hammels project was issued by SCC.

By early 1957 a sponsor had been found, and work on the projects seemed about to begin, although relations between FHA and the city were still troubled. May 1 was set as the date for land acquisition. The Chamber argued that this date was unrealistic and that the community should be allowed to make arrangements for 1957 summer rentals. In February, Lebwohl of SCC wrote a memo suggesting that condemnation be delayed till after the summer: "I believe, in view of the continued requests of Wolpert, the Rockaway Associations and the owners, we should announce the delay in getting final approvals of the plans for these projects as due to delays on plan processing and FHA questions involved in mortgages." [31] Moses agreed. He wrote to the president of the Chamber acknowledging that the May date was unrealistic and postponing condemnation till September 15.[32]

During the summer of 1957, Moses and FHA became involved in a battle over the Lincoln Square project, which caused a delay in all other projects, and Moses stated that the Rockaway projects would probably not be started until early 1958. The Chamber of Commerce advised owners on the sites to make rentals for the summer of 1958.[33]

The Chamber's advice proved to be sound, for Moses ran into still another roadblock. In November, 1957, FHA informed Moses that it would not insure mortgages for Hammels because the project would not be a safe investment at the monthly rentals of $38–$40 a room that the developer planned to ask.[34] Moses decided to seek an abatement of city taxes on the project, thereby allowing the developer to charge lower rents and thus meeting the objections of FHA.

To obtain tax abatement for the project, Moses had to seek the approval of the Board of Estimate. There he met opposition from two sources—City Controller Lawrence Gerosa and Queens Borough President James Crisona. Gerosa had previously stated his opposition to any tax abatement. His natural conservatism was reinforced by his position as guardian of the city treasury, and he looked most unfavorably upon any proposal that he thought would lessen city revenues. Crisona was also a fiscal conservative, and he objected to the proposed abatement on the same grounds as Gerosa.

The Chamber of Commerce of the Rockaways was ideologically indistinguishable from Crisona and Gerosa. It also had an added reason for disliking tax abatement for the projects. The higher the rent in the new projects, the higher the prestige of the Rockaways and the more potential business there would be for the members of the Chamber. It thus came out against tax abatement. Moses made it clear to Chamber officials, however, that the choice was not between a project with tax abatement or without it but between a tax-abated project and no project at all. From the Chamber's point of view, anything was an improvement over what existed in the Hammels area. Early in December they announced a reversal of their position, stating that they would support Moses' request for tax abatement.[35]

Late in February, 1958, Moses informed Wolpert that condemnation would definitely not take place until after the 1958 summer season.[36] In November, 1958, Crisona was elected to a judgeship. Although he was not to leave the Borough Presidency until January 1, 1959, the Board of Estimate managed to overcome his opposition to tax abatement. His farewell words were given at the November 21 hearing of the Board, where he charged that the tax exemption represented a "$21,000,000 giveaway" of city funds.[37] This prompted Wolpert to write Crisona a letter objecting to his desire to delay the projects.

Other progress was made during 1958 aside from resolving the tax-abatement issue. In August the Zukerman Brothers were named as tentative sponsors for both projects, in November CPC approved the preliminary plans for the projects, and in December the Board of Estimate gave its approval. On January 13, 1959, the final plans for both projects were approved by CPC.

In February, 1959, what had now become an annual ceremony again took place. Wolpert wrote to Lebwohl suggesting that landlords on the Seaside site be permitted to lease property from the sponsor (who, it was presumed, would by then have title to the sites), so that they could get another summer of rentals. Lebwohl favored the idea of allowing Seaside owners another season, in part because it would lessen the opposition of the owners to the projects. Moses, however, on Lebwohl's memo supporting the proposal for another season, scrawled, "I am dead against this. The answer is NO once and for all." [38]

Events were again to nullify Moses' decision. On March 12, 1959, the projects were given final approval by the Board of Estimate, and in April the federal government granted a total of $8 million for the two projects.[39] HHFA was not completely satisfied, however, with Moses' handling of the information about the projects. In particular, it was unhappy about what was considered the looseness of Moses' figures on the value of the land to be condemned. It refused to allow title to be vested until individual parcel-by-parcel appraisals had been made of both sites. This was a lengthy process. Amid the usual exchange of charges between SCC and the federal government, condemnation was delayed till after the summer of 1959.

The Hammels property owners had now been subjected to five years' delay. Their patience and their pocketbooks were wearing thin. The area was steadily deteriorating, maintenance costs were becoming higher, and it was becoming almost impossible for the owners to obtain insurance on their property. When it was announced that the property would not be taken till after the summer of 1959, the Rockaway Beach Property Owners and Civic Association, to which a majority of the affected owners in Hammels belonged, announced that it would take legal action to compel the city to take title to the land. Violet Star, the executive secretary of the Association, stated, "Since the first announcement of the projects, owners of land scheduled for condemnation have suffered loss of income, deterioration of property, and the strain of uncertainty." [40] In the beginning of September, the Association, backed by the Edgemere Civic As-

sociation and the Chamber of Commerce, moved in City Court
to compel the city to take title.

At the same time that the court case was instituted, the Chamber of Commerce took other steps. Assemblyman J. Lewis Fox, whose district included the Rockaways and who was chairman of the Chamber's Legislative Committee, wrote to Walter Fried, the director of HHFA for the New York region. He stressed the importance of immediate condemnation of Hammels and said that Moses had suggested in a letter to Fried ways that condemnation could be speeded up but that Fried had not replied. Moses, who was getting quite impatient himself, had apparently worked through the Chamber to apply pressure to the federal government. On September 10, Fox, Wolpert, and David Koss, the 1959 president of the Chamber, met with Fried and with Sam Brooks of the SCC staff. Fried agreed to certain moves to expedite title-taking.

In October, 1959, SCC qualified two sponsors—Zukerman Brothers and the Frouge Construction Company—to bid for the building of the projects. The qualifying of two sponsors was greeted with much enthusiasm by observers of the Title I program because it represented the first time that there was to be competition for the building of a project. The enthusiasm was short-lived. The New York *Post* charged that Frouge had been represented by several influential political figures in his attempt to be named as a potential bidder. On October 31, Frouge withdrew, and two days later the Seaside and Hammels properties were sold to Zukerman Brothers.

Even the official naming of the Zukermans as sponsors was not without controversy. They had been represented in their bid for the sponsorship by George T. Grace, an associate of Sidney Baron. Baron had served as contact man for Carmine DeSapio, chairman of the New York County Democratic Committee, and for many other figures in the Democratic Party in connection with real estate and construction matters. On the day that the sale was made to the Zukermans, the city discovered that S. J. Kessler and Sons, an architectural firm, had been retained by the Zukermans to design the two projects. The Kessler firm had been barred by the city from doing any further work on slum clearance because of their connection with the Manhattantown scandal, but the sale went through. Mayor Wagner, apparently referring to the suit of the Rockaway Beach property owners, stated that the city could be sued if it delayed the sale. Finally, J. Clarence Davies, Jr., the city's Commissioner of Real Estate, announced that he would oppose Zukerman's hiring of the Urban Relocation Company to do the relocation work on the two projects. Davies said that Urban Relocation already had too much work to handle and that it had been criticized for its job on the Penn Station South project. Moses favored the naming of the Urban Relocation Company but said that he would support Davies, the person responsible for overseeing relocation.[41] The Zukermans agreed not to hire Urban Relocation.

There was one last battle over 1960 summer rentals in Seaside. Several owners of property on the site began court proceedings to compel the city to allow temporary renting of their premises. The Chamber of Commerce supported this move, probably because those suing were members of the Chamber. The Rockaway Council of Civic Associations opposed the Chamber. It offered to provide the city with legal assistance to prevent 1960 rentals.[42] The Association feared that the reopening of the many bars in Seaside would have adverse effects on the surrounding area. The city did not accept the Association's offer of assistance, and it proved unnecessary. The court case was lost, and no rentals took place. By the summer of 1960, demolition was already under way.

While the Chamber of Commerce and the civic associations were concerning themselves with the timing of the land condemnation, the Negro community of Hammels became involved in a fight over whether its largest church would be torn down when demolition began.

St. John Baptist Church was an important institution in Hammels. It had a membership of over 800. Its pastor was the Reverend J. A. Jackson, and among its influential members was Leonard Scarbrough, the political leader of the community.

The church had been located at 145 Beach-81st Street, but it was condemned to make way for the Hammels public housing project. In February, 1953, the church had filed plans to build a new building to be located on Beach-82nd Street, near the oceanfront. The plans were approved by the Department of Buildings, and in April construction began.[43] In February, 1956, the handsome brick structure was completed, having cost a total of about $180,000.

The construction of the church had already begun when news of the proposed urban renewal projects was released. Despite the fact that the new building was located within the boundaries of the Hammels site, the congregation decided to continue construction. Jackson later stated, "We had been assured that if our church was up and standing before the city started to buy the land in that area, that we could stay. It was on that basis that we in all good faith built." [44] Whether Jackson ever received such an assurance is not known. Scarbrough did write to Moses in September, 1954, inquiring as to what plans had been made for the church.[45]

On November 13, 1956, SCC issued a booklet containing the architect's plans for the Hammels project. Two churches on the site, St. Rose of Lima Catholic church and Temple Israel synagogue, both on Beach-84th Street, were marked as being excluded from demolition. St. John's was not. Jackson wrote immediately to Moses protesting, in a rather mild and restrained fashion, the proposed demolition of the new church.

In February Scarbrough began a letter-writing campaign. He wrote to Moses and sent a copy of his letter to HHFA, asking them not to approve the plans for the project until St. John's was permitted to stay. Scarbrough's letter touched on the theme of prejudice and also struck a minor chord of religious appeal:

It is true that we are NEGROS but we need a place to wishope [sic] just as well as anybody else, and we would like to be on the OCEAN front as well as the rest of the people. . . . THANK you all and may GOD ever BLESS you. I remain yours as ever in CHRIST our LORD.

YOUR Brother,   L. E. SCARBROUGH [46]

To this appeal he received a short note from Lebwohl saying that it was not possible to save the church.[47]

At the same time Scarbrough also penned a Biblical appeal to Joseph McMurray, the State Commissioner of Housing and a resident of the Rockaways. He wrote to

pray asking you to help us save our church from the wrath of those who seek to destroy it [and to] allow our church to remain as they did with the two WHITE CHURCHES, and we pray to GOD with GREAT hope that you with your great authority will join with us in this FIGHT.[48]

For the next few months Scarbrough wrote to an ever-widening circle of influentials. He wrote to various local and state officials, to Emanuel Celler and other New York congress-men, and to President Eisenhower. Most of the letters sent to federal officials and congressmen were forwarded to the Federal Urban Renewal Commissioner, who waited till he had collected them all and then sent them on to Walter Fried, the Regional Director of HHFA. Although eloquent, the letters were not very specific. The Urban Renewal Commissioner was under the impression that St. John's was located in the Park Row urban renewal project.[49]

Congressman Celler, since the church was in his district, showed some concern. He wrote to Moses asking his reaction and views to Scarbrough's most recent letter. Moses replied to Celler that the church had been built even though the congrega-tion had been aware that it was within the urban renewal site and that the congregation had not approached SCC until the building had been completed. Moses also pointed out that the church had been offered two possible sites for relocating, but that Scarbrough had turned them down.[50]

Celler's inquiry to Moses was a routine one. It represented the usual move of a congressman who receives a complaint from a constituent about something over which the congressman has no direct control. But Scarbrough's campaign had some effects that were not so routine. In June, Charles J. Horan, the Regional Director of the Urban Renewal Administration, wrote to Lebwohl citing the newness of the St. John's building and the cost to the government of acquiring the church property:

Should you deem it necessary in your planning for this project to acquire and demolish this church, strong justification must be given for so doing. Would you kindly give this matter your immediate attention and respond to this letter as quickly as practicable.[51]

Lebwohl replied, defending the decision to condemn the church because of the necessity for closing off Beach-82nd Street.[52]

In May, 1958, Edward Botwin of the SCC staff came up with a new proposal. He mentioned the vigorous protests of the church to various officials and the reluctance of the congregation to move off the site. He suggested moving the church to Beach-84th Street, placing it between St. Rose of Lima and the synagogue: "Its removal from B82nd Street will precipitate allegations of racial and religious discrimination which may hinder final approval of the project. These will be groundless if Beach 84th Street can be planned as 'Church Row.' "[53] Nothing came of this proposal.

On October 9, 1958, a week before CPC was to hold public hearings on the two projects, the Reverend Mr. Jackson wrote to CPC for the first time. He also sent copies of his letter to the Board of Estimate. The letter urged that the church not be torn down. Felt replied that it was too late for CPC to do anything, since it had already adopted a report recommending approval of the project. He assured Jackson, however, that the Board of Estimate would give consideration to the church's views.[54]

On October 28 the congregation and Board of Trustees of St. John's passed a resolution "praying" that the church be spared from demolition. The resolution was sent to SCC, but a quick change of heart occurred. A few days later Stephen Wardell, the chairman of the church's board, and Jackson met with Brooks and Lebwohl of SCC. Borough President Crisona was also present and served as mediator. Agreement was reached on relocating the church to a site on Beach-74th Street, and in early November the church's board voted to accept this offer.

On November 6 Moses issued a press release "to correct misapprehensions which have found their way into the press about the treatment of the Church of St. John Baptist." He explained that the church had been offered another site, that it would be generously compensated, and that if it had been located on Beach-84th Street, it would not have been slated for demolition.

The issue of St. John's seemed to be settled, but late in 1961 Jackson died. He was replaced by the Reverend Robert Sitton, who reopened the whole relocation controversy. Sitton renewed the charges that the city was discriminating against the Negroes and demanded that St. John's receive a larger plot of land than the Beach-74th Street site that had been agreed upon. The reasons Sitton reopened the whole question are obscure, but two facts may be relevant. First, about four months after Sitton became pastor, he had a falling-out with Scarbrough. Scarbrough then tried to get the congregation to unseat Sitton but failed. The new battle over relocation may have been part of the power struggle between Scarbrough and Sitton. Second, Sitton instituted court proceedings against Scarbrough and Assemblyman Fox, the church's attorney, to recover control over the money that the church had received from the city as a condemnation award. Whether the dispute over the condemnation money was a cause or a result of the dispute between Sitton and Scarbrough is not known. Nor is it known whether or how Scarbrough and Jackson's original decision to accept the Beach-74 Street site and Sitton's later decision to dispute this agreement were influenced by the condemnation money.

The original publicity over St. John's had attracted the interest of the Protestant Council of the City of New York. The executive secretary of the Council, the Reverend Leland E. Gartrell, wrote to the SCC's architects to inquire about the church. Gartrell kept an eye on events in the Rockaways, but it was not until March, 1962, when the controversy was reopened, that he saw an opportunity for the Council to be of service. Gartrell arranged for Samuel Ratensky of HRB to meet with Sitton to discuss the matter. On the date of the meeting, Sitton failed to show up. Another date was arranged, and this time Sitton, Gartrell, and the Reverend Grant Anderson, executive director of the Queens Federation of Churches, all met in Ratensky's office. The meeting accomplished nothing, however; Sitton could not be reasoned with and insisted upon making the central question the charge of racial prejudice.

Eventually, the city managed to get Sitton to accept the Beach-74th Street relocation site. As of this writing, the church is still standing and is the only building remaining on the Hammels site. Presumably, it will be torn down soon, and, if the money is available, a new church will be built at Beach-74th Street.

The relocation of St. John Baptist Church primarily concerned the Negro community of Hammels. In 1960, when everything except relocation seemed to be settled, there arose a dispute in which the Negro community had no particular interest but which aroused the feelings of some of the leaders of the civic associations. This dispute was over the proposed height of the buildings in the two projects.

The original plans had called for the buildings to be eight

stories high. Early in 1960 the sponsors, with Moses' approval, submitted a revised plan that called for doubling the height of the buildings, increasing them to sixteen stories.

Some of the civic associations objected vehemently to the proposed change. Their objections were based primarily on the additional noise that would be caused by planes taking off from nearby Idlewild (now Kennedy) Airport. If the buildings were built to sixteen stories, they would be the highest structures in the Rockaways, and planes taking off from the airport would have to climb more steeply, thus creating more noise. The civic associations also seemed to fear that the planes might fly more directly over their respective areas in order to avoid flying over Seaside or Hammels.

The regional manager of the Federal Aviation Agency wrote to CPC urging it to delay approval of the increased height because of the possible increase in noise.[55] At the CPC hearing on October 11, 1960, this view was taken by individual Rockaway property owners and residents and also by Jules Michaelis, president of the Wavecrest Civic Association and the Rockaway Council of Civic Associations. Michaelis was particularly vehement because, aside from the noise issue, he was afraid that the sponsors would construct additional buildings on the open space gained from increasing the height of the buildings. This additional construction would increase the density of the projects, a possibility that the civic associations did not want to encourage.

The sponsors of the projects and a representative of the Rockaway Chamber of Commerce appeared at the hearing in favor of the proposed revision. The Chamber made it clear that if any government agency presented any valid objections to the increased height, it would go on record as also opposing the increase. It stated, however, that it favored the increase "because higher buildings represent progress in this community." [56]

Following the CPC hearing, considerable infighting took place among the Rockaway organizations. I. Bernard Hirsch, the new executive secretary of the Chamber of Commerce, wrote to Felt, the chairman of the Planning Commission:

The City Planning Commission itself has been misled by objections raised by alleged "representatives of the Rockaway Community." One person in particular who purports to represent the thinking of the Rockaway Council of Civic Associations has distorted the actual position of this group on this problem. Many of the civic associations in this group do not object to these buildings and have taken a position similar to ours. If necessary, we can supply you with written documentation of their stand.[57]

Meanwhile, someone mobilized additional support for the Chamber by getting Father Joseph Tschantz of St. Rose of Lima Church and Rabbi Gabriel Beer of Temple Israel to write Felt favoring sixteen-story buildings because of the increased open space that this change would permit.[58] Michaelis, in turn, found a way to snipe at the Chamber. He submitted to Felt petitions from the St. Joseph and the Peninsula hospitals objecting to the amount of noise in the Rockaways. Michaelis was careful to point out that among the signers of the Peninsula Hospital petition was George Wolpert, then the executive secretary of the Chamber.[59]

On November 23, 1960, CPC issued its report. It recommended a Solomon-like compromise that limited the height of the buildings to twelve stories. This recommendation was accepted by the Board of Estimate, and the building height was set at twelve stories.

Relocation and Code Enforcement. The fact that the Hammels site was inhabited largely by low-income Negroes was never forgotten by the participants in the various controversies over the projects. As it became certain that the projects would actually be built, the community leaders focused increasingly on the problem of what was going to happen to the people on the site.

There are no exact figures of the actual number of families

that were on the Title I sites. In November, 1959, SCC officially counted 1,763 families on the Hammels site alone.[60] In June, 1961, the New York *Post* said there had been 1,223 families in Hammels and 155 in Seaside.[61] In a final tally, the City's Department of Relocation could account for 967 families in Hammels and 142 in Seaside.[62] This problem in statistics reflects the large number of people who moved without the assistance, or even the awareness, of city authorities.

Aside from the Negro community itself, those who were most directly concerned about the possible effects of relocation from Hammels were the civic associations of the neighborhoods, which feared that "undesirables" would relocate in their area. As early as April, 1954, when the site of the project was still being debated, the Edgemere Civic Association held a meeting to discuss the possible effects of relocation. *The Wave* reported that the Edgemere residents were "alarmed at prospects of Edgemere becoming 'Welfare town.' " [63] In November, 1956, the Somerville-Arverne Civic Association wrote to Moses expressing its concern about relocation from Hammels. It stated that it did not want a repetition of what had happened when the Hammel public housing project was built, and that it did not want "undesirables" in its neighborhood.[64]

In the fall of 1958, when the projects were ready for CPC approval, the fate of the site residents became a prominent issue for the first time. The first skirmish concerned the role of the City Welfare Department, which had been blamed by many in the community for helping to create the existing Hammels slum. Early in September, the Chamber of Commerce, representing a group of property owners south of Hammels (Beach-56th Street to Beach-61st Street), sent petitions signed by about fifty persons to the city. The petitions charged that the Department of Welfare was calling property owners in the area, seeking to have them convert their summer properties to year-round use so that persons on relief could be installed as tenants. The Welfare

Department wrote back to Wolpert saying that it was a violation of department policy to make such calls and that the Department staff had denied making them. Furthermore, said the letter, the Department staff had been instructed not to solicit housing in the Rockaways since 1954.[65]

The concern about relocation increased. Later in September, Michaelis, a man with influence in the Borough President's office, wrote to Moses. Michaelis stated that his organization was "greatly worried as to where the 5,000 residents of the Hammels and Seaside area will be relocated" and that it feared "that our neighborhood and everything we stand for will be lost." [66]

The concern of the Rockaway residents also became the concern of Queens Borough President Crisona. On October 3 Crisona asked the Board of Estimate to have the city's Urban Renewal Board do a redevelopment study of the entire Rockaway Peninsula. He further asked that the city acquire for renewal and redevelopment a 4-mile strip of land between Beach-35th Street and Beach-115th Street, that the housing codes be tightened and rigidly enforced, and that the procedures of the Department of Welfare be studied because they had resulted in an excessive flow of welfare cases into the Rockaway area.[67] Most of this statement seemed like a grandstand play to capture the approval of the Rockaway audience. The Urban Renewal Board was not created to make studies and was not equipped to do them. The proposal to condemn more than eighty square blocks was unrealistic. The Board of Estimate turned the matter over to the Urban Renewal Board, which pointed out these shortcomings, and the matter was dropped.

As the date of title-taking was delayed till after the summer of 1959, the question of relocation subsided into the background. Finally, in the fall of 1959, the city condemned the property and sold it to the sponsors. At about this time, the Rockaway Health Council called a meeting of various community leaders and organizations, including the civic associations, the P-TAs, the

American Jewish Committee, and NAACP. The result of this meeting was the formation of the Rockaway Council for Relocation and Slum Prevention, with the Reverend Joseph May, a Negro, as chairman. The Council was to be the major voice of those on the Peninsula who, while wanting to prevent slums, also wanted to protect the Negro community from abuses.

The fate of the Negro community came to citywide attention nine days after the city had sold the land to the sponsors. On November 11 a prominent article (headed "Rockaway Residents Face Need for 2nd Move From a Slum Site") appeared with accompanying photographs in the New York *Times*. The substance of the article was an interview with Leonard Scarbrough, leader of the low-income Negroes. It described his political and economic stake in the community and the previous moves that the Negroes had been forced to make from the site of the public housing projects. It then quoted Scarbrough as saying, "From 74th Street on it's all white now, the same as it was on this side of Rockaway Boulevard before they built Hammel Houses. We don't expect any more trouble moving down there than we did moving in here." Scarbrough explained that members of the St. John's congregation had already purchased three rooming houses in the area: "They're right on the edge of the beach, where everyone has to go past to get to the water. If we have trouble we'll fill them with undesirables, and don't you worry—the white people will move out fast. That's just how we did it here." [68]

Scarbrough's statements did not come as a surprise to the civic associations and other groups in the Rockaways. Everyone concerned knew that there was a battle on, and the publication of the strategies of one side did little to change the picture. The only major effect of the Scarbrough interview was to bring an additional force into the struggle. After reading the interview, J. Anthony Panuch, who was in the process of doing a major housing study for the Mayor, asked the Commission on Intergroup

Relations (COIR) to investigate Scarbrough and his tactics. This assignment was accepted by COIR but not quite in the spirit Panuch had anticipated. COIR was an official city body, but it had almost no powers except those of investigation. Its staff consisted mostly of Negroes and Puerto Ricans, and its primary function was actually to serve as a pressure group acting to defend minorities. COIR investigated the situation in the Rockaways and rapidly aligned itself with the Council for Relocation and Slum Prevention, providing them with as much assistance as its limited powers would permit. Rather than finding fault with the tactics of Scarbrough, COIR concluded that the major Rockaway problems were

(1) insufficient standard housing to absorb the site tenants; (2) opposition by local "civic associations" to Negroes moving in; (3) inability of the organized sympathetic community (Rockaway Council for Relocation and Slum Prevention) to help; (4) questionable tactics on the part of the relocators in pressuring families to move, especially out of Hammels, though they wanted to stay; (5) real estate interests and "operators" taking advantage of the families' plight; (6) no agency taking the responsibility to help.[69]

The Rockaway Council for Relocation and Slum Prevention was handicapped in its efforts by the lack of adequate staff and funds and also by a lack of any official standing or access to public officials. This last problem was overcome to some extent by the Council's cooperation with COIR. During its first few months the Council was also hampered by a lack of internal cohesion. It had attempted to be broadly representative of the Rockaway community, and its original membership included a number of representatives from the civic associations. These representatives lacked sympathy for the basic orientation of the Council, and they were soon to leave the Council for an organization more to their liking.

Early in January, 1960, John Clancy, who the year before had succeeded Crisona as Borough President, announced the formation of a Borough President's "Watchdog Committee" for slum prevention in the Rockaways. At first the Committee was simply designed to coordinate the work of the various city departments, and it consisted only of representatives of the departments. The civic associations, however, unhappy with the Relocation Council, demanded representation on the Borough President's Committee. Clancy thus appointed a number of civic association people to the Committee and made Michaelis chairman of the Committee. No representatives of the Relocation Council or the Chamber of Commerce were appointed. The civic associations resigned from the Council for Relocation soon after they joined the "Watchdog Committee."

The "Watchdog Committee" was not a success. Its meetings tended to be somewhat chaotic, and nothing ever seemed to be resolved. The city departments had little desire to be coordinated, and the civic associations were continuously preoccupied with scrapping among themselves. Clancy never showed up at the meetings, and his representatives only rarely made an appearance. Michaelis used the same tactics he had adopted in his other organizations and soon assumed the right to speak in the name of the Committee. His relationship with Clancy seems to have been based on their mutual usefulness to each other. Michaelis enjoyed the prestige of being the Borough President's man and also hoped that Clancy would in some way reward him for being chairman. Clancy probably figured that he was gaining good publicity from the statements that Michaelis issued. Eventually, however, Michaelis began to feel that Clancy might be using him as a scapegoat for the bad conditions in the Rockaways.

The "Watchdog Committee" concerned itself primarily with code enforcement. They informed the City Buildings Department and the Fire Department of possible violations and in this way attempted to control and prevent the shift of the Hammels Negroes to other locations in the Rockaways. This rather nega-

tive approach reflected the basic concern of the civic associations, which was to keep the Negroes out of the white areas.

In March, 1960, the Council for Relocation, the local chapter
of NAACP, and the Chamber of Commerce joined in denounc-
ing relocation practices. They stated that many of the site
tenants were being moved into wooden summer houses which
had been hastily and inadequately converted for year-round
use.[70] The major agitation about relocation did not begin, however, until the winter of 1960. By mid-November 372 families
had been relocated, 63 of them into substandard quarters.[71]

On November 18, the "Watchdog Committee" held a special
meeting to consider the spread of slums in the Rockaways. The
committee was under pressure both from the residents of the
areas near Hammels and from the mass media. The director of a
new cooperative housing project in Arverne said that many of
the residents of the co-op were "close to panic" because of the
potential down-grading of the surrounding area.[72] Both the
Journal-American and the *World-Telegram & Sun* ran articles
charging that there had been a worsening of housing conditions
due to relocation from Hammels. The Committee succeeded in
getting the Department of Buildings to make a house-by-house
inspection of the area around Hammels.

Meanwhile, Scarbrough was making his voice heard. He
wrote several letters to Mayor Wagner, to the newspapers, and
to J. Clarence Davies, Jr., the head of the newly created Housing and Redevelopment Board, which had assumed responsibility for the projects. Scarbrough charged that the Watchdog
Committee was simply trying to get rid of the Negroes, and he
referred to Michaelis as "John Casper the Second." Scarbrough's
accusations, however, had only a limited effect. The newspapers
were more inclined to listen to the "community leaders" on the
Watchdog Committee than to the spokesman for a depressed
Negro neighborhood. The story was not "big news" in any case.
The staff of HRB kept track of the Hammels situation, but

Scarbrough's innumerable charges and his single-minded pre-occupation with discrimination dulled the effect of any new accusations. Scarbrough's effect was further lessened by the suspicion of HRB that he was primarily concerned with finding housing on the Rockaways for the Negroes because of his real estate interests and because of the money that would come to him in finder's fees.[73]

The battle over the Negroes continued throughout 1961. In January Edward Lewis of the Urban League arranged an appointment for Mrs. Rausnitz of the Relocation Council to talk to Borough President Clancy. He told Clancy that Mrs. Rausnitz and the Reverend Mr. May thought that the "Watchdog Committee" was unrepresentative of the community and biased in its actions. Clancy thereupon appointed Mrs. Rausnitz, the Reverend Mr. May, and I. Bernard Hirsch of the Chamber of Commerce to the committee.

On March 9, COIR, which had again increased its activities in the Hammels area, invited the project sponsors and a number of city officials to a meeting in its office to discuss the Hammels situation. The meeting was primarily a response to the plight of the approximately 300 families who still remained on the Hammels site, many of them without heat, water, and other necessities. During the winter two children on the site had died of pneumonia. The Zukerman Brothers were concerned simply with getting the remaining tenants off the site as fast as possible. Each of the city departments disclaimed responsibility for the situation. The COIR meeting failed to reach any agreement on improving relocation or on bettering conditions on the Hammels site, and the city departments were resentful at having been called to a formal meeting for such a purpose.

Another move of COIR's was more successful. It prevailed upon Ellen Tarry, an intergroup relations specialist for HHFA, to make an inspection trip to Hammels. Miss Tarry made several trips to the site during March and was shocked by what she saw.

Her first report to the regional director of HHFA was rejected as being too partisan. Her visits did, however, result in an improvement in some relocation practices.

During the remainder of 1961 two significant actions were taken to prevent slums in the Rockaways. The first of these was the city's designation of Arverne, the neighborhood just east of Hammels, as an Area Services Project. This move received the approval of both the "Watchdog Committee" and the Relocation Council. Both organizations, however, were soon to become unhappy about the Services Project. Part of the council's unhappiness related to the second effort to prevent slums.

This second move was the introduction in the City Council by Eric Treulich, representing the Rockaways, of a bill to prevent the conversion of summer houses to all year-round dwelling places. The bill was clearly aimed at those buildings, primarily in Arverne, that were being converted to provide rooms for Negroes displaced from the Hammels project and for other Negroes and Puerto Ricans coming to the Rockaways. There are two ways in which one can judge this bill. The Council for Relocation and the Queens Federation of Churches concluded that anything which decreased the housing supply for minority groups on the Rockaways was bad and could result only in worsening housing conditions. They therefore opposed the bill. The city administration, including Leon Schneider, the director of the Arverne Area Services Project, believed that no good could come of increasing the supply of bad housing on the Rockaways and thus supported the bill.

The Treulich Bill was passed in 1962. So far it has had no real effect because its validity is still being tested in the courts. The controversy over the bill, however, had the effect of cooling relations between the Council for Relocation and the Area Services Project. In addition to the split on the Treulich Bill, the Council was disappointed with the efforts the Services Project was making to prevent slums. The Project was supposed to coordinate the efforts of all city departments concerned with housing and focus them on one area. In actuality, the project achieved little more coordination or action than had existed before. The split between the Council and the Services Project resulted in an almost complete lack of communication between the city agency and the group of citizens who were most sympathetic to the city's viewpoint.

By the end of 1961 the two sites had been completely cleared of tenants. According to the official figures,[74] 618 families were relocated into standard apartments, 133 were relocated into substandard apartments, and the fate of 271 families is unknown. Almost all the families from Seaside stayed in Queens. Of the 967 families in Hammels, 546 stayed in Queens, 310 went to Brooklyn, and the other 111 relocated either outside the city or in other boroughs. It was widely reported that the large number of Hammels tenants who relocated in Brooklyn were placed in apartments in the Brownsville area, one of the city's worst slums.

The battle over relocation entered a new phase, focusing on the efforts of the Negroes to establish themselves in Arverne. Everyone in the Rockaways had anticipated this problem, and the efforts to get the city to establish the Arverne Area Services Project had been an attempt to meet it. The Arverne situation was brought to the notice of the citywide Negro community by a banner headline in the *Amsterdam News* of December 30, 1961, which declared, "We Traded One Slum Home for Another." The article was based mostly on quotations from the Reverend Mr. May of the Council for Relocation.

The Borough President's "Watchdog Committee," headed by Michaelis, attempted to meet the situation by putting pressure on the city's Department of Buildings to enforce the housing codes. The Committee hoped that this strategy would prevent the conversion of houses into additional quarters for Negroes.

The "Watchdog Committee" had been hurt, however, by the creation of the Area Services Project. Its monopoly on official standing and access had been destroyed. No longer could it claim to be the only official body concerned with the Arverne situation. Its influence over which buildings were to be inspected was transferred to the Area Services Project. This change was highlighted in March, 1962, by Michaelis' resignation as chairman of the Committee. He attributed his resignation to the fact that the Committee had been bypassed by the Area Services Project, and he denounced the project as "a flop." [75] He later said that he had resigned because corruption in the city departments made it impossible to improve the Rockaway situation.[76]

Scarbrough, meanwhile, continued his fight to hold the Negro community together and to keep it in the Rockaways. As the dimensions of the housing problem in Arverne became apparent, talk spread of another urban renewal project. It seemed that the whole process of renewal and relocation might take place again, one step further down the Peninsula. Scarbrough proclaimed himself ready for this eventuality:

If the area is taken by the city and Negroes and Puerto Ricans are not properly housed on the ocean front then we will continue to move into the next area, on and on to Far Rockaway, Woodmere, Cedarhurst, Lawrence, and on out as far as land lasts, we must have decent housing and where we want it. You may make all the laws you wish, you may send all the harassing inspectors you wish, but we vow we will live on the ocean front if there is houses to live in.[77]

OVERVIEW AND REPERCUSSIONS

As of this writing, construction of both Seaside and Hammels is about half completed, and sponsorship of the project has again changed hands. What has been the overall effect of the two projects?

From a purely physical standpoint, there has undoubtedly been an improvement. Whatever may be the architectural and social shortcomings of the projects, they represent a vast improvement over the miserable slums of Hammels. This improvement is somewhat mitigated by the fact that the refugees from the Hammels site probably speeded the deterioration of the Arverne area. The degree to which the deterioration has been accelerated is impossible to measure, but the conversion of summer bungalows to year-round dwelling places and the splitting-up of former private houses into one-room boarding houses give clear indication that the area is deteriorating. On November 5, 1964, CPC designated all of Arverne as "appropriate for urban renewal."

The social effects of the projects and of the controversies connected with them are much harder to evaluate. It seems clear that there has been an increase in what is loosely called "community tension." The conflict between white and Negroes has been intensified. In June, 1962, at the initiative of Lovevine Freamon, Jr., president of the Queens branch and State Housing Chairman of NAACP, two meetings were held to discuss what Freamon called the "explosive situation" in the Rockaways. Mrs. Rausnitz and the Reverend Mr. May were the main speakers at the first meeting. Freamon listed four factors responsible for the Rockaway situation:

(1) displacement of minority groups from site after site for public housing construction or Title One development; (2) failure of humane and adequate relocation procedures for them; (3) inability to achieve approval of new public vest pocket housing; (4) rejection by the majority group of the minority groups from most private housing.[78]

The Negroes have once again been uprooted and have again had to go through the process of trying to reestablish community ties. The needs of the multiproblem family, that oppressed segment of society too wretched to qualify for public housing, remain unmet. Once again they seem to have been propelled into their aimless wandering from renewal site to renewal site. The fact that they may bear, in part, the responsibility for creating their own environment does not lessen the need to find some way to alleviate the problem.

Scarbrough seems to have been successful in reestablishing the base of his power in the low-income segment of the Negro community. The Arverne-Hammels Democratic Club did not suffer any significant drop in membership and has found a new building for its headquarters. St. John Baptist Church, however, did lose a significant percentage of its congregation (about 25 percent), and the leadership of the church has been thrown into doubt by the clash between Scarbrough and the minister, the Reverend Mr. Sitton. Of the Negro families on the Hammels site, over 500 were relocated in the Rockaways.[79] Not many of them went into public housing. Generally speaking, Scarbrough has made good his threat to "march down the peninsula."

For the white community, the problem of the Negro has become even more prominent and inescapable than it was. This is obviously true for the people of Arverne, who are faced with all the conflicts and uncertainties of living in a changing neighborhood. In the rest of the community the split between the "liberals" and the other groups has been accentuated, and the opposition of the property owners to public housing on the Rockaways has stiffened and become more ardent.[80]

There was no single renewal controversy in the Rockaways. Rather, as we have seen, there was a series of disputes involving different issues and different actors, but all the disputes were related to the construction of the Title I projects. The large number of groups on the Peninsula and the deep divisions that existed among them probably account in part for the fact that the city's action caused so many distinct issues to arise—the site of the projects, the date of title-taking, the relocation of St. John's, the height of the buildings, and the relocation of the Hammels Negroes. This pattern of numerous separate disputes contrasts sharply with the "shape of the issue" in the West Village, which we shall describe in the next chapter.

CHAPTER IV

The West Village

Greenwich Village has always been an area set apart from the rest of New York. Its separateness is apparent from a glance at a street map (Figure 2). As the neat rectangular gridiron pattern of Manhattan nears Washington Square from the north, it is suddenly fragmented into a maze of narrow crooked streets, many still bearing old historic names, like Christopher, Bleecker, Barrow, and Sullivan.

For more than fifty years the Village has been well known as the "Bohemian" section of New York, but the population of the area—which extends from Fourteenth Street to West Houston Street and from Fourth Avenue to the Hudson River—does not and has never consisted primarily of artists, "beatniks," or others associated with the Bohemian life. The Village has been subject to many of the same population shifts as the rest of the city. A small colony of Scottish weavers had settled there by the end of the eighteenth century,[1] but the first major immigrant group to settle in the Village came from Ireland in four distinct waves in the nineteenth century. In the 1880s a large number of Italians settled in the area. Smaller groups of Spaniards, Jews, and Germans also found a home in the Village.[2]

Around the turn of the century, the artists who were to give the Village its Bohemian reputation began to settle there. The migration of the artists to the Village probably reached its peak

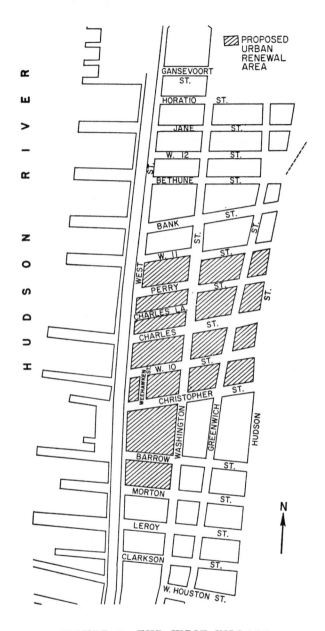

FIGURE 2. THE WEST VILLAGE

in the 1920s,[3] but the area is still a Mecca to many artists from all over the country.

Following World War I came the greatest migration to the Village—a movement that today is still continuing at a rapid pace. It consisted of middle-class Americans, mainly professionals, who moved to the Village because its reputation appealed to them and because good housing could be found there.

The juxtaposition of the Bohemian reputation and the middle-class migration created two themes that run through the life of the community from the 1920s on. The first of these might be called the defense of Bohemian values, about which the Village middle class was as ardent as the artists. Such values included a tolerance for individuality of all sorts and a belief in the central importance of artistic and intellectual pursuits. These beliefs resulted in a certain alienation from and distrust of the larger American society because of its failure to subscribe to the same general value scheme.

The other theme, which has been repeated constantly for the past forty years, is that "the Village is changing" and that the spirit of the Village is thus being destroyed. This cry was raised by the artists against the middle class and by the middle class of the 1920s and 1930s against the succeeding middle class of the 1940s and 1950s. The ancient vintage of the charge does not detract from its validity—the Village has changed constantly and is still changing.

These two themes have tended to intermingle in the past few years. The changes taking place in the Village have been interpreted as a manifestation of the crass outer world attempting to impose a commercial uniformity on the artistic individualism of the Village. Since about 1950, the people of the Village have been involved in one fight after another against private developers and city agencies who wish to build apartments or widen streets or change traffic patterns. Washington Square, Verrazzano Street, Hudson Street, Simkhovitch Houses, Washington Square Village—all have been battles in defense of the

Village way of life. The Villagers have lost only one of these battles, that over the construction of the Washington Square Village Title I project. These high-rise, high-rent apartment buildings south of Washington Square stand as a symbol to many Villagers of the evil of urban renewal.

The middle class has not been alone in its battles to preserve the Village. The Italian community, the second largest group in the area, has also had its share of combat. The Italians were once the dominant group in the Village, but in recent years they have lost strength as the second and third generations have moved to the suburbs and to other parts of the city.

Since about 1940 the needs and wishes of the Italians have been expressed through the Democratic Party rather than through civic organizations. A number of small Italian clubs and organizations do exist, but they are primarily social in nature. In 1951, however, these social groups combined to form the Lower West Side Civic League. The impetus for the formation of the League was the battle against South Village, an urban renewal project proposed by Moses' Slum Clearance Committee. The project would have destroyed a large part of the Italian community. The South Village project was defeated, and a few years later the League played an important part in defeating the plan for Simkhovitch Houses, another project that would have made serious inroads on the Italian area of the Village. The League is primarily a "holding organization" and generally does not take a stand on any issue that might divide the Italian community.

There is a certain amount of conflict between the Italians and the middle-class professionals. In 1956 a new community newspaper, the *Village Voice*, was founded as a rival to the *Villager*. The *Villager* gave much space to the Italian community and focused on events that were primarily of interest to Greenwich Village. The *Voice*, on the other hand, was aimed at the middle class. It contained a number of articles and features designed to interest those throughout the city and the nation who considered themselves a part of the intellectual *avant-garde*. One observer remarked bitterly that the founding of the *Village Voice* symbolized the "suburbanization" of the Village.[4]

The major conflict between the middle class and the Italians has taken place within the Democratic Party. Greenwich Village was the home base for Carmine DeSapio, who was the leader of the New York County Democratic organization, better known as Tammany Hall. In 1957 the Village Independent Democrats was established as a rival to DeSapio's Tamawa Club. The VID grew out of the 1956 Greenwich Village Stevenson for President Committee and was part of the Reform movement that has been attempting to gain control of the Democratic Party throughout the city. The VID aimed to strike at the heart of the regular party leadership by ousting DeSapio, the symbol of evil for all the Reformers.

The VID, like the rest of the Reform movement, was supported primarily by middle-class professionals.[5] In the Village the Italian community rallied to the support of DeSapio, who had pioneered the way for the Italians' seizure of power from the Irish. In 1957 VID's Herman Greitzer ran against DeSapio for District Leader and polled 36 percent of the vote. In 1959 the VID ran Charles McGuiness, who obtained 47 percent of the votes cast.[6] In 1961, the Reformers, running on the same primary ticket as Mayor Wagner, elected James S. Lanigan and Carol Greitzer as District Leaders.

The political battle has affected the other major organization in the Village, the Greenwich Village Association (GVA), which is probably the most representative group in the Village. Its membership includes most of the leaders from both the Italian and middle-class segments of the community. The sharpening of differences caused by the political battle resulted, however, in numerous charges that the association was controlled by the old-guard Italians, while others charged that it was being seized by the Reformers.

In February, 1961, the attention of the Village was temporarily diverted from party politics to urban renewal. The city announced its interest in constructing a housing project in that area of the Village traditionally known as the West Village.

The West Village, which consists generally of the area west of Hudson Street and Eighth Avenue between Christopher and Fourteenth Streets, has shared in the changes that have affected the Village as a whole. Its nearness to the waterfront, however, has resulted in certain differences. The population has tended to remain Irish, the Italian community being centered further to the east. Much of the land is occupied by industry. Residential construction has lagged considerably behind the Village as a whole, and most of the residential development has taken the form of converting old buildings rather than constructing new ones.

The site in the West Village that the city proposed to study for urban renewal was bounded by West Eleventh Street, Hudson Street, Christopher Street, Washington Street, Morton Street, and West Street. Of the land on the sixteen-block area, 78 percent is devoted to nonresidential uses such as factories, truck transfer depots, and warehouses. According to the 1960 U.S. Census of Housing, 42 percent of the housing units in the area were deteriorating or dilapidated, and the Planning Commission estimated that 40 percent of the nonresidential structures were in poor condition.[7] About half of the housing units in bad condition are accounted for by three hotels and one rooming house in the area. A survey by the West Villagers reported that all dwelling units in the area had running water, cooking facilities, and private toilets.[8] About 3 percent of the dwelling units are owner-occupied.[9]

According to the 1960 census, 1,741 people live in the area.[10] About 25 percent of these are Puerto Rican, while between a third and half are Irish Catholic, and most of the rest are Protestant and Jewish professionals. The study done by the West

Villagers stated that 50 percent of the families in the area earned $5,000 or more per year.[11]

If the figures leave a vague picture of what the area is like, it is only because the area is itself a mixture of good things and bad, of ugly old factories and tenements next to charming renovated houses. Many of the inhabitants of the area maintain that it is precisely this mixture which makes the West Village a desirable place to live, but to many outsiders the area remains a slum, a blighted section of the city.

Prior to the fight over the urban renewal project, the West Village was notably lacking in neighborhood organizations. One group of property owners—the Greenwich Village West Council—did exist. The Council had been formed in 1959 by a small group of owners on Jane Street and West Twelfth Street, a few blocks north of the urban renewal study site. Its main purposes were to keep trucking on the streets to a minimum, to protect and plant trees, and to improve garbage collection in the area. In 1960 the leadership of the Council was taken over by Dr. Donald Dodelson, a young dentist whose home and office are located on Jane Street in a building he has bought and renovated. Dr. Dodelson expanded the organization to cover the entire West Village. In 1961 it had about eighty or ninety members, although only a few were actively interested in the Council's activities.

There were two churches on or near the West Village site. St. Veronica's, a Catholic church, was attended primarily by the Irish population. St. Luke's Chapel, part of Trinity Parish, served the Protestant portion of the community. Some members of St. Veronica's Parish had disliked the idea of worshipping with Puerto Ricans, while St. Luke's, with a long tradition as a missionary chapel, made efforts to attract the newcomers. Nestor Berrios was the major figure in St. Luke's efforts to make contact with the Puerto Rican community.

Most of the West Villagers considered the area a part of Greenwich Village. The community-minded residents were members of Village organizations, read the Village papers, and participated in Village activities. Although a part of the Second and Third Assembly Districts, when the West Villagers sought political advice or assistance, they usually turned to the clubs and leaders of the First Assembly District, which covered the rest of Greenwich Village. The lack of organizations rooted in the West Village was indicative of the degree to which the West Villagers identified with the Village as a whole. When the time came for the West Villagers to do battle with the city government, their close ties to Village organizations proved to be an important asset.

THE WEST VILLAGE PROJECT

The City Acts. Greenwich Village both needed and wanted middle-income housing, or so it seemed to city officials and other outside observers. In October, 1958, the opposing candidates for Congress, the State Senate, and the State Assembly from the Village area spoke at a meeting of the Washington Square Business and Professional Women's Club. The dominant theme running through all their talks was the need for middle-income housing "to help preserve the pattern of the Washington Square area and Greenwich Village" and "to keep middle-income families from moving to the suburbs." [12]

The Greenwich Village Association, the most representative organization in the area, was quite ardent about obtaining middle-income housing. Whitney North Seymour, Jr., chairman of GVA's housing committee, stated in May, 1959, that his committee hoped to encourage low- and middle-income housing in the area west of Hudson Street on the eight blocks from Christopher to Jane Streets. [13] In December the housing committee published a brochure designed to attract sponsors for

government-aided housing projects. In April, 1960, the new
chairman of the housing committee, Norman Redlich, wrote a
letter to J. Clarence Davies, Jr., chairman of the Housing and
Redevelopment Board, requesting a meeting to discuss the possibility of obtaining middle-income housing for the Village.[14]

During the summer of 1960 the possibility of obtaining such
housing came close to realization with the announcement by two
different groups that they were willing and anxious to be the
sponsors of a middle-income project. Redlich, representing
GVA, had been meeting for several months with New York
University, the Borough President's local planning board, the
Lower West Side Civic League, and the Washington Square
Association. In July Redlich wrote to HRB: "We feel that our
preliminary discussions have now reached the point where we
would like formally to request that our organizations be considered as applicants for joint sponsorship of a middle-income
cooperative housing project in the Greenwich Village area." [15]
Three possible sites for the project (none of them in the West
Village) were described in the letter. Davies replied that two of
the sites were unsuitable and that the third was under consideration by another group. "However," said Davies, "we are as interested in finding a site that is suitable and possible for middle-
income housing in the Village as you are and will do everything
within our power to find something we can begin work on in
the immediate future." [16]

The other group that Davies mentioned as having one of the
sites under consideration was the Middle-Income Co-operators
of Greenwich Village, better known as "Micove." This group
was formed by Charlotte Schwab, a housewife who lived in the
Village. Having been frustrated in her search for a new apartment, she decided to take action and formed a group whose sole
purpose was to sponsor a middle-income project in the Village
area. By June, 1960, the organization had obtained a membership
of several hundred. It was having meetings, holding fund-raising

affairs, and conducting guided tours of housing projects. As a
site for the proposed project, it had settled on a twelve-block
area bounded by West Broadway, Broome Street, Broadway,
and Houston Street. Micove also selected a noted architect, Vic-
tor Gruen, to draw up plans for the project.[17]

Mayor Wagner added his voice to those who wanted a middle-income project in the Village. In September, 1960, the Board
of Estimate voted to allow New York University to take over
part of the Washington Square Village Title I site. A number of
Village leaders objected to this, claiming that the housing needs
of Greenwich Village outweighed the needs of the university.
Just prior to the Board's vote, Wagner made a statement designed to meet these objections:

The Board of Estimate is aware that this will not solve the middle-
income housing needs of Greenwich Village. . . . We are therefore also directing the city's Housing and Redevelopment Board
to continue its efforts to plan and provide for the construction of
additional middle-income housing in the area.[18]

By November, 1960, the efforts of HRB had resulted in the
selection of the West Village site as the best location for a
middle-income project. Davies, along with James Felt of the
City Planning Commission, had inspected the site and CPC had
given its informal approval.[19] Within HRB, however, it was referred to as "Fried Village" because Walter Fried, a member of
HRB, had first suggested the site.

The site was chosen for several reasons. The project would
provide an opportunity to separate industrial buildings from
residences, thereby eliminating heavy trucking from residential
areas. The project could also simplify the rather chaotic traffic
pattern that exists in the area. Furthermore, a number of major
changes were anticipated in the West Village area, and it was
hoped that the project would help to shape the future nature of
the community. The dismantling of an elevated railroad spur,
the abandonment of a large but antiquated federal office build-

ing, and the departure of a large wholesale market were among
the changes HRB hoped could be utilized to make the West
Village a more attractive community. Work on a General
Neighborhood Renewal Plan for Greenwich Village was to be
started at the same time as the project.[20]

The Board noted that the Neighborhood Renewal Plan would
pay particular attention to

(a) The salvage and conservation of any structures which give
the area its unique character. (b) The preservation of any structures which have been or can be rehabilitated to serve a useful
purpose compatible with a logical plan for the area. (c) The preservation of the flavor and mixture, ethnic, social, and economic, which
have made Greenwich Village a desirable residential area for New
Yorkers and for continuing generations of adopted New Yorkers.
(d) The feasibility of developing one of the adjacent piers for
recreational uses.[21]

HRB was not the first group that had picked the West Village
site. As has been mentioned, GVA's Housing Committee had
named the same area as the logical place for a project. But even
before this, in May, 1950, Moses had considered putting a project in the West Village.[22] He rejected the idea because "the
demolition of houses and removal of tenants would arouse
storms of protest." [23]

HRB, however, anticipated no such opposition. It did not
consider itself a proponent of the Moses bulldozer approach, and
it had promised to mix conservation and rehabilitation along
with new construction.[24] It felt that it was fulfilling a desire of
the community by providing middle-income housing. This feeling was confirmed by the favorable reaction HRB received
when, prior to publicly announcing the site, it checked in-
formally with several local leaders.

HRB submitted its request for planning funds to the Board of
Estimate on Wednesday, February 15, 1961.[25] The request was
for $300,000 from the federal government to finance a detailed

survey of the site and the drawing up of plans for the project. That the proposal was not first officially submitted to CPC for hearings and approval was unusual and later became a point of great controversy.

Public announcement of the project was made the following Monday by both Wagner and Davies. Another project, Tompkins Square, on the lower East Side, was announced at the same time. The press releases stated that the tentative idea for West Village was to construct middle-income housing east of Washington Street and to leave the area west of Washington Street for industrial uses. Davies was also quoted as saying that the area was predominantly blighted but that the project would "strive to maintain the general character of the surrounding community while eliminating those elements that have tended to cause blight." [26]

The newspapers carried the press releases on Tuesday. Wednesday was Washington's Birthday, a public holiday. On Thursday the Board of Estimate was scheduled to meet to give its approval to the request for planning funds. In this short period between the public announcement and the Board of Estimate meeting, the West Village began to mobilize.

The Community Mobilizes. One of the people on the West Village site whom HRB did not consult was Jane Jacobs. Mrs. Jacobs was the mother of three children and an assistant editor of the magazine *Architectural Forum.* She had moved to New York from Scranton, Pennsylvania, in the 1930s. In 1948 she and her husband, an architect, purchased a house in the West Village. Soon afterward Mrs. Jacobs began to take an active part in Village affairs. In 1955 she was appointed vice-chairman of the Greenwich Village Study, a group of Villagers who organized to formulate plans for the physical improvement of the area. Mrs. Jacobs acquired experience in dealing with the city when the members of the study decided to fight the proposed opening of Washington Square to traffic and also when she succeeded in preventing the city from widening Hudson Street, which ran in front of her home.

By February, 1961, Mrs. Jacobs had substantially completed work on a book devoted to a biting condemnation of current practices in city planning, housing, and urban renewal.[27] One of the main themes in the book was the importance of neighborhoods in city life and the need for neighborhoods to have a voice in deciding their own destiny. When Mrs. Jacobs read in the paper that the city was requesting planning and survey funds for the West Village, it seemed to her that the neighborhood was endangered by all the evils about which she had been writing.

The evening of February 21, Mrs. Jacobs and her husband attended a regular meeting of GVA. A number of important Village leaders were present at the meeting. Several of them had been informed about the project by HRB and had reacted favorably. When the regular evening meeting was finished, however, Mrs. Jacobs cornered as many of the leaders as she could and tried to convince them that no good could come of the city's request for funds. Being a very persuasive woman, she convinced most of them that at least they ought to request a month's delay so that the proposal could be considered by the neighborhood. The next day, Wednesday, Mrs. Jacobs called some of her friends and several other Village leaders and also convinced them that a delay should be requested.

When the Board of Estimate met on Thursday to approve HRB's request, thirty-two residents of the West Village and State Assemblyman Passannante were there to object. The members of the Board of Estimate, other than the Mayor, knew nothing about the project and summoned Walter Fried of HRB for an explanation. Davies had left for a vacation in California. Fried said that no project plans had been made and that the request for funds was simply to provide money for a survey on which to base such plans. The West Villagers accused Fried of "evasiveness." They pointed out that the request specifically mentioned a "project" and even gave it a name.[28] Passannante urged the Board of Estimate to delay its decision in order to give the community time to study the proposal. He also said that Greenwich Village was a "high-cost neighborhood" and that private industry could do the job.[29] The Board postponed action on HRB's application for one month. The Tompkins Square application, which had been submitted at the same time, passed without trouble.

The West Village leaders now had a month before any further action would be taken by the city. They wasted no time in organizing themselves. On Saturday night, two days after the Board of Estimate meeting, 300 people crowded into the auditorium of St. Luke's School to form a committee to fight the city proposal. Mrs. Jacobs had decided that it would be best to utilize the one existing organization in the West Village, Dr. Dodelson's Greenwich Village West Council, as a base from which to begin their mobilization.

At the Saturday night meeting the Committee to Save the West Village (CSWV) was formed as a committee of the Greenwich Village West Council. Mrs. Jacobs and Dr. Dodelson were named co-chairmen.[30] Fifty-four residents of the area signed up to contribute their time and effort to work for the committee. Mrs. Jacobs stated that the CSWV's aim "is to kill this project entirely because if it goes through it can mean only the destruction of the community." [31]

The general line that CSWV and other opponents of the project were to take was established at the time of the first Board of Estimate meeting and was largely the handiwork of Mrs. Jacobs. It was based primarily on two points: first, that the city government could not be trusted and, second, that the West Village was not "blighted" and should be preserved *in toto*. The opponents mistrusted the city government on almost every point. They claimed that the timing of the Board of Estimate hearing was undemocratic and designed to railroad the project through before the neighborhood could say anything. They claimed that the city was not just requesting funds for planning but that it already had specific plans for a West Village project and simply wanted the money to get started. The opponents also gave no credence to the city officials' statement that any project in the area would combine conservation and rehabilitation with new construction. They were convinced, or at least said they were convinced, that a project meant "total destruction."

Mistrust of the city gave the movement emotional fuel with which to fight its battle, but the other argument—that the West Village was not a blighted area—gave CSWV a chance to put its activists to work. The Committee set about organizing a house-by-house survey of the site area to try to prove that it was a well-integrated community with few slums or tenements.

A martial spirit pervaded CSWV. Mrs. Jacobs' house became the "general headquarters," and a local restaurant, the Lion's Head, became the "command post." A communications network, consisting of children and housewives in the area, was set up to report to the command post if any strangers appeared in the area. Mrs. Jacobs gathered around her a corps of skilled young professionals—Erik Wensberg, the editor of the Columbia University *Forum*; Stephen Zoll, an editor for the Macmillan Company; Pierre Tonachel, a real estate attorney for a Wall Street firm; Hugh Byfield, a physicist; H. William Nudorf, a research expert for the advertising agency, Batten, Barton, Durstine and Osborn; and Rachele Wall, a professional public relations expert. Each was put to work utilizing his respective skills.

But it was not enough to recruit the middle-class professionals. The committee had to obtain the solid backing of the neighborhood so that the charge could not be made that only one segment of the community was opposed to urban renewal. Leon Seidel, the proprietor of the Lion's Head, was helpful in getting the support of some of the small local businessmen.

There remained the large segment of Irish Catholics and the approximately 100 Puerto Rican families.

Contact with at least a portion of the Puerto Ricans was not difficult. Nestor Berrios, one of the Puerto Rican leaders, was an old friend of Mrs. Jacobs' and had attended the first meeting at which the committee was organized. He succeeded in getting several other Puerto Ricans to work for the cause.

The Irish Catholics proved more of a problem. A valuable recruit was obtained when Mr. Jacobs persuaded Danny Lough-lan, the proprietor of one of the local bars, to attend the initial organizational meeting. The major institution in the Irish segment of the community, however, was St. Veronica's Church. The regular pastor of the church was quite old and feeble, and the actual running of the church was in the hands of Monsignor Edward Head. Monsignor Head was a good friend of Roger Schafer, one of the moving spirits behind Micove, and was favorably disposed to an urban renewal project. According to Mrs. Jacobs, Monsignor Head did not take an immediate stand on the city's move, because he was not the official pastor of the church and did not feel that he represented the opinions of the parish as a whole. John Six, a parishioner of St. Veronica's and a member of CSWV, circulated petitions opposing the city's actions throughout the parish, and enough signatures were collected to counteract any stand that Monsignor Head might take and thus to insure the appearance of neighborhood unity.

Within a few weeks after the Mayor's announcement, Mrs. Jacobs had thus succeeded in organizing a committee that had strong neighborhood support, in gathering around her a group of highly skilled and sophisticated lieutenants, and in insuring that there would be no significant dissenting voices from any portion of the West Village. She had also obtained the backing of most of the leaders of the larger Greenwich Village community. It was clear that if the city government chose to fight, it would have a major battle on its hands.

The Lines Are Drawn. The issue having become centered on the good faith of HRB and CPC, Davies and Felt believed that as a matter of principle they could not retreat. Also, they were both convinced that if the request for planning funds was turned down because of neighborhood pressure, it would mean the destruction of the urban renewal program in New York. Davies stated this fear explicitly: "I am not exaggerating when I say that all of us here are firm in our fear that, if opposition is allowed to stop this study from being made, the entire urban renewal program in the City of New York is in danger." [32]

With the battle on, both sides rapidly acquired allies. Some of these allies were sought out by the major participants; others were rather unwelcome. The first group to jump into the fray was Micove. On March 2 Micove's attorney wrote to Davies requesting that the organization be named as the tentative sponsor of the West Village project. He explained that the organization also still wanted sponsorship of the original Houston Street site, "inasmuch as the present [West Village] site cannot fill the housing needs of Greenwich Village residents." [33] As it became public that Micove wanted to sponsor the proposed project, rumor began to spread in the Village that Micove had already obtained the sponsorship and was simply part of the whole city plot to deceive the West Village. Fried was forced to issue a statement saying that although HRB had consulted with Micove prior to announcing the West Village project, Micove had definitely not been promised any sponsorship.[34]

Micove was not content with simply requesting sponsorship of the proposed project. Soon after the official city announcement, Mrs. Schwab set up a subsidiary committee, the West Greenwich Village Site Tenants' Committee, to support HRB against the onslaughts of CSWV.[35] The Site Tenants' Committee was supposed to represent Micove members residing in the West Village. How many such people there were is difficult to estimate. On March 2 Micove claimed there were "approximately one hundred." [36] By March 14 this had grown to "hundreds," [37] and by March 27 the organization was claiming 500 applicants in the project area.[38] The original estimate of 100 was probably exaggerated. On March 5 Micove held a meeting in the West Village to convince the residents that rehabilitation and redevelopment would be a good thing. According to the *Village Voice*, "The audience response in the form of catcalls, boos, and indignant speeches proved the attempt to be conspicuously unsuccessful." [39]

Samuel Ratensky, projects director for HRB, also spoke at the March 5 meeting. The Villagers' suspicion that Micove was a tool of HRB was reinforced by the fact that a high HRB official had spoken at a Micove-sponsored meeting. By the end of the month HRB began to think that Micove was more of a handicap than a help. The community relations expert for HRB stated in a memorandum on March 27, "The Micove leadership has been fanning the flames with almost every move they have made. . . . It is my feeling that we cannot afford to have Micove act as our defender." [40] Micove seemed to be effectively alienating all other organizations in the Village. It was subject to general mistrust because of its "undemocratic" nature. It had been formed as a corporation to build apartments, not as a representative group to speak for its members. Mrs. Schwab and the other directors spoke in the name of the group, but there was in fact no formal way in which the rank-and-file membership could participate in decisions or make its opinions known. The other organizations that wanted to sponsor housing in the Village thought that Micove had behaved irresponsibly in announcing its plans for a co-op before having an approved site. The group's exaggerated claims of support and Mrs. Schwab's tactical errors added to the general hostility felt toward Micove.[41]

During March HRB acquired another ally who was more

welcome although perhaps less useful. This was the Citizens
Housing and Planning Council, a citywide group consisting of
the more liberal real estate men, planners, and others interested
in the field of housing. Davies, the chairman of HRB, was a past
president of CHPC and had been closely associated with it for a
long time. The Council had had a previous dispute with Mrs.
Jacobs over the issue of closing Washington Square to traffic.
On March 26 the CHPC Board of Directors voted to support
the proposal for a survey of the West Village area. Mrs. Jacobs
responded by charging that CHPC had acted upon inadequate
information and that some of the members of CHPC's board
were biased because of financial stakes in the outcome of the
controversy.

While CHPC and Micove sided with the city, most of the
organizations in Greenwich Village wasted little time in aligning
themselves with Mrs. Jacobs. Shortly after the announcement of
the project, a group of prominent Villagers—Norman Redlich,
Barbara Reach, and Anthony Dapolito of GVA, and William
Passannante, the State Assemblyman for the Village—went to
see Walter Fried of HRB. They asked for assurances that there
would not be total clearance on the West Village site. Fried
pointed out that the general policy of HRB and its specific statements concerning the Neighborhood Renewal Plan for Greenwich Village supported conservation of sound housing. He
stated, however, that since there was no plan for West Village
(what the city was requesting was funds to draw up a plan) and
HRB had no detailed knowledge of the area, he could not give
any guarantees about the extent of clearance. The Villagers decided that they could not support the proposal on this basis.

On March 13 GVA came out against the request for planning
and survey funds. GVA was the first Village-wide group to take
such a stand. It objected to the haste of the city's proceedings
and to "the upheaval threatened by this proposal." It requested
that HRB meet with community organizations to find possibili-

ties for housing in Greenwich Village that would involve a minimum of relocation.⁴² The day after GVA took its stand, the Borough President's Local Planning Board also voted against the city proposal.

The West Villagers acquired a strange bedfellow on March 20, when the Real Estate Board of New York announced that it was against the city's request for funds. The Board of Governors approved a resolution of its Housing Projects Committee, stating that the city's request should be opposed "on the ground that private enterprise has demonstrated its willingness and ability to rehabilitate this area to such an extent that the intervention of a government-aided project is not warranted." ⁴³ This endorsement was somewhat embarrassing to the Villagers, in view of the fact that one of their main cries for many years had been that the Village was being ruined by high-cost apartment buildings being constructed by private developers. Part of the Villagers' opposition to urban renewal was based on the fact that rents charged in renewal projects were too high and therefore had the same injurious effect as private construction.

On March 23 VID, after listening to a debate between Fried and Mrs. Jacobs, passed a resolution opposing the city's plans for West Village. The club based its opposition on the grounds that the project would require tenant relocation. Sarah Schoenkopf, a leading VID member, stated in the club's newsletter, "We don't have to tear down people's homes in order to put up homes for other people." ⁴⁴

VID had a large membership and was quite active in Village affairs, although it had not yet achieved designation as the official Democratic club in the area. This could be accomplished only by the defeat of DeSapio at the polls in a primary election. In 1959 VID had come close to defeating DeSapio, and it was now focusing all its efforts on the September, 1961, primaries, where it would once again have a chance to expel the party leader. The West Village was not in the same Assembly District as the VID, but by this time there was little doubt that the general sentiment of the Greenwich Village population was against HRB and with the West Villagers.

In addition to VID, other local politicians also sided with the West Villagers. As was related earlier, William Passannante, Assemblyman for the First Assembly District, was one of the first to oppose the request for planning funds. On March 14 Louis DeSalvio, Assemblyman for the Second Assembly District, telegraphed Fried urging cancellation of the project. He charged that community and civic groups in the area had been "completely ignored," that HRB's action was "unilateral and arbitrary," and that the choice of the area "for demolition" had been carried out in secrecy.[45] Leonard Farbstein, the Congressman for a large part of the Village, including the West Village, strongly implied that he also sided with the West Villagers. He was quite annoyed that he had not been consulted by HRB beforehand and requested that "hereafter I would be advised prior to the board taking action on any projects in my Congressional District." [46]

The solidarity of Greenwich Village leaders in backing CSWV had effects outside of the Village. Many of these leaders were also influential members of citywide groups. A number of groups that might have supported the city took no stand because of the divided opinion among their own leaders. Thus, the influence of such Village leaders as Stanley Tankel and Bob Weinberg on the Citizens Union, Barbara Reach on the Community Service Society, and Juliet Bartlett on the Women's City Club persuaded these organizations to take no stand on the controversy.

Since the immediate issue was whether the Board of Estimate would approve HRB's request, the most important community representative in the situation, other than the Mayor, was Edward Dudley, the Borough President of Manhattan. Dudley owed his position as Borough President to the influence of Mayor Wagner.[47] The West Village controversy placed him in the unhappy position of having to choose between the man responsible for his appointment and a large number of the constituents who would be responsible for deciding whether to reelect him. In this situation Dudley did what any good politician would—he delayed.

On March 16, Dudley announced that he would ask the Board of Estimate to postpone consideration of West Village for five weeks while Mayor Wagner recovered from an ear operation.[48] On March 21 he spent an hour and a half inspecting the West Village and then submitted to an hour of questioning from neighborhood residents. He refused to concede that the city had erred in calling for urban renewal, although he stated that he was impressed by the high standards of the area. Concerning the request for planning and survey funds, he said, "I think if your arguments are cogent enough, the Board of Estimate might set it aside." [49]

On March 23 the Board of Estimate met and, in accordance with Dudley's wishes, action on West Village was postponed until April 27. Several hundred West Villagers attended the meeting, having been brought there by buses that CSWV had rented for the occasion. Representatives of CSWV tried to persuade the Board to kill the proposed plan outright, but they were unsuccessful. One month more was allowed both the West Villagers and HRB to pursue the battle. Both sides proceeded to do so.

Maneuvers. Early in April, Davies, who had been upset by the lack of newspaper support for HRB's position, asked William Ogden of the New York *Times* to have lunch with him so that he could explain HRB's stand. Davies followed up the luncheon talk by writing a long letter to Ogden expanding his views.[50] Whether as a result of this talk or not, on May 3 the *Times* did come out editorially in favor of the request for planning and survey funds. The editorial did not cite Mrs. Jacobs by name and did not specifically mention the West Village, but it stated,

If people immediately mobilize, with all the apparatus of demonstration and vilification, whenever an area is mentioned for study—protesting and refusing all possible change for the better without even knowing what may later be decided upon—there is no hope for a better way. The city cannot surrender to the loudest voice and abandon all prospect of reversing the blight of the neighborhood slipping downhill.[51]

Meanwhile, Mayor Wagner announced that when the Board of Estimate met on April 27, he would request that the West Village plan be sent back to CPC for proper processing. This proposal would eliminate one of the major points of criticism, namely, that HRB had acted illegally in sending the proposal directly to the Board of Estimate rather than first allowing CPC to hold hearings and give its approval. Sending the proposal back to CPC would also give the Mayor more time to determine how strong public sentiment was on the issue. It was, after all, an election year.

Two days before the Board of Estimate meeting, Micove sent a letter to all its applicants:

As soon as there is a definite hearing date set by the New York City Planning Commission, you will be notified. At that time it will be necessary for each and every member of Micove to be present at the hearing to prove their need for low and middle-income housing. In spite of highly organized and well-financed opposition to the cause of low and middle-income housing Micove has proved itself stronger than ever.[52]

The letter also urged the membership to write to Mayor Wagner and to Planning Commissioner Felt favoring the West Village plan. Mrs. Schwab later wrote a letter to the New York *Times* declaring, "Over 1,200 individual Villagers are on record as having written Borough President Dudley favoring the study.

Over three hundred of these were from the general area of the West Village." [53]

CSWV was probably more successful in its letter-writing campaign than was Micove. It kept a steady stream of correspondence flowing into the Mayor's office. In the first week of April the Mayor received about 150 letters, mostly from residents within or near the site area, all protesting against a project.[54]

Efforts were also taken to deflate Micove's claims. Five residents of West Village ran an advertisement in both the *Villager* and the *Village Voice*. "Attention Micove Applicants!" it read. "We are Micove applicants who are also members of the Committee to Save the West Village. We wish to make public our disapproval of Micove's backing of the West Village Urban Renewal Project." [55]

Mrs. Jacobs decided that the best strategy for taking advantage of the backing she had received from Greenwich Village leaders was to create a special organization whose sole purpose would be to impress City Hall with the strength and solidarity of her support. Late in April she formed the Joint Village Committee to Defeat the West Village Proposal and Get a Proper One. Anthony Dapolito, the president of the Greenwich Village Association, was appointed chairman of the new group. Mrs. Jacobs decided that, since Dapolito was a Democrat, the vice-chairman should be a member of the local Republican club. Carey Vennema, a captain in MacNeil Mitchell's Republican organization, was thus appointed to the second slot. Dapolito was a DeSapio supporter, however, and James Lanigan, the president of VID, left the first meeting of the new organization when he discovered that Dapolito was to lead it. The Joint Committee was not intended to be a working body and it never was. It fulfilled its role simply by coming into existence and thereby giving publicity to the support CSWV had from Village leaders.

On April 27 the Board of Estimate met at City Hall. What took place is probably best described in the account which appeared in the next day's *Herald Tribune*. Paul Screvane, the Deputy Mayor, was sitting in for Wagner. He

announced to a packed room that the Board would refer the urban renewal project back to the City Planning Commission for more study. Up jumped H. Marshall Scolnick, an engineer representing the West Greenwich Villagers. He contended that any action taken by the board was illegal, that those in opposition wanted to be heard. Mr. Screvane said the Greenwich Villagers would not have to stay around since the item had been returned to the commission. When Mr. Scolnick persisted in getting the arguments heard, Mr. Screvane began lecturing him and the partisan audience. Finally, the room quieted down, Mr. Scolnick preparing hmiself to jump up again when the item came up for a vote of referral. The board took on the heavy calendar. As the Greenwich Village item grew closer, tension increased in the room. Then, the eight board members approved sending the request back to the Planning Commission. The board moved on to the next item. Mr. Scolnick shouted. Other Greenwich Villagers yelled. "It's being illegally sent back to the City Planning Commission," Mr. Scolnick shouted. "We want to be heard. They're 7,000 people living in the area." "You're not going to be heard," Mr. Screvane said. Here Assemblyman Louis DiSalvio, a lower West Side Democrat, joined in the argument but the board moved on to the other items. Mr. Scolnick continued to stand in front of the board. Suddenly, after the board had acted on several more items, Mr. Scolnick informed the board members, who now had been joined by Mayor Wagner, that he had a court order to serve. He gave one copy to a Board of Estimate clerk and then, opening the gate to the press well which is directly below the board's dais, he approached the Mayor and gave another copy to him.[56]

The court order the Mayor received directed CPC, HRB, and the Mayor to show cause why they should not be restrained from designating the West Greenwich Village area as "blighted." The "blighted" designation was a necessary prerequisite to an application for planning and survey funds, and the state general municipal law [57] required that public hearings be held before an area could be designated as blighted. The West Villagers' case was based upon the fact that no such hearings had been held. The order was dismissed on May 15 by Justice Greenberg of the State Supreme Court on the grounds that the question had become academic, since CPC was now going to hold public hearings on the plan. He noted, however, that, "As a simple matter of justice, equity and public decency, there is considerable merit to the plaintiff's position." [58]

The issue of West Village now focused on CPC, which was dominated by its chairman, James Felt. Felt was a close personal friend of Davies' and he believed just as strongly as did Davies that the whole future of urban renewal in New York depended upon overcoming the opposition of the West Villagers.

The CPC's hearing was scheduled for June 7. Felt spent the month of May campaigning for approval of the city's request for planning funds. On May 1 CPC issued a report on urban renewal progress, in which Felt promised that new safeguards developed by HRB and CPC would be applied in full to any West Village project.[59] On May 7 he assured the Village residents that the city wanted to retain the "flavor" of the Village, that the bulldozer approach was never intended, and that the area would not be demolished.[60] On May 8 he issued a statement saying that urban renewal presents great opportunities and must now work to preserve neighborhoods. He said that the West Village criticism was "misguided" because "well-meaning, sensible citizens rebelling against our architecture, our technology, our mores and our culture in general have sought to single out urban renewal as the villain." [61]

On May 9 Felt, at his own request, spoke to the City Council to outline his plans for urban renewal in 1961–62. He emphasized his opposition to the bulldozer approach and the efforts that CPC was making to preserve neighborhoods. The councilmen were delighted that a member of the administration should take the trouble to speak to them about his plans.[62]

That evening Felt ventured deep into enemy territory and spoke before a skeptical and frequently hostile audience at Greenwich House, located only a few blocks from the West Village site. He repeated that the bulldozer approach would not be used in any West Village project. Six nights later he again spoke at Greenwich House defending the city government's procedures and intentions. The *Village Voice* described him as "angry" and the audience as "even angrier." [63]

Polemics and Politics. The CPC hearing on June 7 turned into a display of the strength of the West Village forces.[64] The hearing began at four o'clock in the afternoon and lasted until four o'clock the next morning. Eighty-one speakers appeared before the commission. Only fourteen of them favored the West Village proposal. Only five members of Micove appeared to speak. A number of other Micove proponents were scheduled to speak, but they never appeared.

The presentation of the West Village's cause was a masterpiece of organization. Each speaker had been assigned a specific topic and limited himself to speaking on that subject. Three lawyers discussed why the city's moves were illegal—one lawyer dealing with municipal law, one with state law, and the third with federal law. An acoustical engineer testified that the West Village had been scientifically proven to be quieter than most other places in the city. A resident read figures from the Department of Air Pollution to prove that the air was cleaner in the West Village. A Puerto Rican resident read figures to prove that the area was integrated. Letters were read from architects, novelists, and artists to prove that urban renewal was an evil and that the West Village was not blighted.

Erik Wensberg, editor of the Columbia University *Forum*,

was primarily responsible for organizing the hearing presentation. He introduced each speaker for the opposition, meanwhile missing no opportunity to point out the dearth of CPC supporters. The two speakers who represented the viewpoint of the Real Estate Board were followed by the strongest speakers on the Village side, so as to minimize the impact of the real estate men. Old-time residents who were poor speakers were given letters to read from those who could not be present at the hearing.

The hearing was somewhat disturbed by another maneuver of CSWV. This was the circulation, during the hearing, of a petition to remove Felt and Davies from office. Some of the more eminent speakers disassociated themselves from any desire to oust Felt or Davies. The petition was handed to Mayor Wagner's secretary, but its only real effect was to make the Villagers appear as extremists to outside groups.

CPC deferred any decision on whether to declare the West Village "blighted." The public hearing had provided little support for the commission's position. Furthermore, the primary elections were only three months away, and, regardless of the outcome of the elections, the city's political picture would be very changed after September. The Democratic Party was dominant in the city, but it had been sharply split. Wagner, the incumbent mayor, had decided to reject the support of most of the regular Party organization. The organization had decided to run Arthur Levitt, the State Controller, against Wagner in the primary. The Reform faction of the Party, which was powerful in Manhattan, came out in favor of Wagner. Meanwhile, the incumbent City Controller, Lawrence Gerosa, announced that he would enter the primary as a third candidate for the mayoralty.

Against this background of political warfare, the West Villagers continued their struggle through the summer. They engaged in activities designed to strengthen their organization. Attempts were made to raise funds by staging an art show and holding a book sale. These affairs also served the purpose of emphasizing the intellectual and cultural climate of the neighborhood.

The contacts the committee had with the communications world were put to good use. The editorial support that the New York *Times* had given to the city was partially counteracted by an article in the paper on June 19. Written by John Sibley, it was a review of HRB's first year of operation. It began, "The city's Housing and Redevelopment Board, at the end of its first year of operation, can look back on a prodigious volume of paper work. But not one brick has been laid in a new project." [65] The article did not mention that it is almost impossible to process and begin construction on a renewal project in one year and that it would certainly be impossible for a new agency to do so.

On July 20 the West Village controversy was brought to nation-wide attention via the pages of the *Saturday Evening Post*. The *Post* ran an editorial headed: " 'Urban Renewal' Can Make an End of a City's Charming Historic Spots." [66] "It may turn out," ran the lead sentence, "that the Teapot Dome Scandal of the sizzling '60's will be Urban Renewal." The article went on to say that the only reason that the West Village was being considered for renewal was because the planners and the politicians had been corrupted by the real estate speculators. Early in October the *Post* followed up on its editorial by publishing an excerpt from Mrs. Jacobs' new book.[67]

The few allies of HRB and CPC realized that somehow they had to strengthen their forces. What was particularly needed was an organization that could claim to represent at least a portion of public opinion in Greenwich Village. As long as the Village appeared to be solidly against the project, there was little chance of its ever being approved. Two attempts were made to form Village-based groups that would support the city.

The first such attempt was initiated by Roger Starr of CHPC. He talked to Alan Rudolph, a Villager and assistant to the dean of the School of Architecture of Pratt Institute. Rudolph indicated interest, and Starr contacted several other influential Villagers in an effort to band them together. He explained his ideas in a letter to Truda Lash of the Citizens Committee for Children:

Whether or not the proposal is defeated, I feel convinced that it will be a long time again before any devoted public servant will consider undertaking a program in the Village as a whole. For this reason I have thought that it is in the best interests of New York Citizens that a group of Villagers able to view proposals calmly and to survey their surroundings with common sense, should form themselves together to take a quiet informed look at what the Planning Commission has been talking about.[68]

Starr's efforts proved to be in vain, and the group never materialized.

The other attempt to break Mrs. Jacobs' monopoly on articulate Village opinion took the form of trying to organize a group in the West Village itself. This effort was undertaken by Micove and particularly by its treasurer, James Kirk. Kirk, a business agent for a local of the longshoreman's union, had lived in the Village for sixty years and had then been evicted by a private developer. He was convinced that the West Village was turning into a luxury area and that the West Villagers' opposition to urban renewal was, in fact, opposition to housing for the "lower classes." Kirk got together with two West Villagers, Tom Quinn, a salesman for an oil company, and William Schierberl, a lawyer. Together they formed "The Neighbors' Committee." The committee circulated leaflets in the area and canvassed the neighborhood to obtain signatures on a petition favoring CPC's study. Within a few days they had collected 170 signatures. Mrs. Jacobs retaliated, however, by obtaining notarized statements from 139 of the 170 signers saying that they had been misled into signing the petition.[69] After this counterattack the Neighbors' Committee was not heard from again.

As the primary election drew closer, the West Village issue became increasingly entangled in the city's political struggle. The Democratic regulars aligned themselves with the West Villagers. DeSapio, a Levitt supporter, was facing a stiff fight for his district leadership in the Village. On August 19 he demanded that Wagner call off the West Village study before the September 7 primary or stand branded as "talking out of both sides of his mouth to garner votes." "There are vast slums where redevelopment is needed," said DeSapio, "but Greenwich Village is not a slum area." [70] On the same day Levitt, Wagner's opponent, pledged that if he were elected, he would scrap the proposed West Village study.[71] H. Marshall Scolnick, an old-time Democratic politician as well as a CSWV member, tried persistently to get CSWV to support Levitt's candidacy publicly. Mrs. Jacobs, however, realizing that this endorsement would only endanger the group, steadily resisted.

Wagner, having started out as an enthusiatic backer of HRB's plan, was pushed more and more into the role of an opponent. On August 18, the Mayor issued a statement, written for him by Felt, which stated that he would "vigorously oppose any study which would contemplate a change in the basic character of Greenwich Village." It was expected that the release would at least give the Mayor a good press, but Mrs. Jacobs received advanced word about the Mayor's release. She called Charles Bennett of the New York *Times* and read to him a statement which called the Mayor's promises "pious platitudes" and which said that if the Mayor really cared about Greenwich Village, he would kill the urban renewal proposal completely. The next day's *Times* gave equal billing to the Mayor and Mrs. Jacobs, with Mrs. Jacobs having the last word.[72]

On August 28 the Mayor told a Village audience that he would see that no one was evicted from his home in connection with new housing projects and that the only Village buildings to be torn down would be unoccupied ones.[73] Nothing but complete capitulation, however, would satisfy the West Villagers. On September 1, Mrs. Jacobs and Mrs. Wall talked to Wagner at his campaign headquarters in the Astor Hotel. They repeated their demand that the city leave the West Village alone. The Mayor hesitated and then agreed, saying that he would first have to inform Felt and Davies. When Felt was told by the Mayor of the decision he was quite upset and argued vehemently, but it was of no avail.

On September 5, the day before the primary, Wagner told the press that he would ask CPC to kill the West Village plan. He was, he said, "deeply concerned and sympathetic with the people of the West Village neighborhood in their desire to conserve and to build constructively upon neighborhood life which is an example of city community life at its healthiest." [74] The next day Wagner, with the support of most of the Reform Democratic clubs in the city, was victorious in the primary. This victory was understood to be tantamount to election in November.

Mopping Up. Wagner's announcement did not put an end to the West Village controversy. CPC had been set up under the City Charter to be independent of the Mayor. Felt and the other commissioners, although appointed by the Mayor, served for eight-year terms, whereas the Mayor only served for four. Felt did not consider himself bound by the dictates of Wagner.

On October 17, Mrs. Jacobs, Mrs. Wall, and four other members of CSWV met again with Wagner. The CSWV representatives reported that the Mayor offered them a deal whereby they would save face for Felt by acquiescing in the "blight" designation and the project would then be killed by the Board of Estimate the following week.[75] Mrs. Jacobs, militant to the end, rejected the offer and said that CSWV would, if necessary, go to court to fight a slum designation. Wagner now simply wanted the whole West Village question to be dropped as quietly and quickly as possible, but Felt would not go along.

The next day, October 18, CPC met in open session and declared the West Village area blighted and suitable for urban renewal. The West Villagers quite literally refused to take this sitting down. They "leaped from their seats and rushed forward.
They shouted that a 'deal' had been made with a builder, that
the Mayor had been 'double-crossed' and that the commission's
action was illegal." Felt

sought vainly to restore order by pounding his gavel. Then he
called on the police to remove the unruly from the room. Despite
that, the shouted protests increased. Mr. Felt then called a recess,
sent for more policemen and left the room, accompanied by the
other members of the Planning Commission. The Villagers remained in their seats, chanting "Down with Felt" until the meeting
resumed nearly an hour later. They began shouting their accusations again as the commission secretary resumed the reading of the
calendar. Policemen escorted several from the room and carried
one man out feet first.[76]

The behavior of the West Villagers brought down upon them
the condemnation of the civic groups. The Citizens Union, the
Women's City Club, the Citizens Committee for Children,
United Neighborhood Houses, and CHPC all joined in deplor-
ing the disturbance at the CPC meeting. Mrs. Jacobs was not
apologetic. "We are not violent," she said at a press conference
that CSWV held the next day. "We were only vocal. We were
terribly alarmed at what is happening in our neighborhood and
our city. We had been ladies and gentlemen and only got pushed
around. So yesterday we protested loudly." [77] She denied later
that the disturbance had been planned ahead of time.

Actually, CPC's designation of the West Village as "blighted"
was in some respects a victory for the West Villagers. The leaders of CSWV had realized that if CPC decided to declare the
area blighted, their chances of ultimate victory lay with the
Mayor keeping his preprimary promise. If they could get CPC
to decide before the November election, they would, if neces-

sary, be able to exercise more leverage over Wagner. CSWV thus tried to hurry things as much as possible and was successful in getting Felt to act before the election.

The Board of Estimate was scheduled to meet on October 26 to decide once again whether to approve HRB's request for planning and survey funds. Wagner's two opponents for the mayoralty, Gerosa and Lefkowitz, had announced their opposition to the project. Gerosa, who was also a member of the Board of Estimate, called the plan "a crime against the people." [78] On October 25 Davies announced that HRB had dropped the project and would not submit the request to the Board of Estimate: "We regard it as city policy not to proceed with this project." [79] On November 7, Wagner was reelected Mayor.

The immediate threat of an urban renewal project was now removed, but the West Villagers were adamant in insisting that the "blight" designation also be revoked. They hired a lawyer, Shirley Fingerhood, to make preparations for a case to prove that the designation was illegal. Even if the case was never brought to court, the CSWV leaders figured that preparation of the case was a good tactic to keep pressure on the Mayor to have Felt remove the designation.

CSWV also began to chip away at CPC's few supporters. In its report on the October 18 meeting, CPC listed as supporters of its action the International Longshoremen's Association, the New York City Central Labor Council, and the New York chapter of Artists' Equity Association. [80] Upon reading the report, Agnes and Danny Loughlan told Mrs. Jacobs that they were sure that the longshoremen would not have voted to support CPC. They suggested that Mrs. Jacobs speak to their friend William P. Lynch, vice-president of ILA. On November 15 Lynch wrote to Felt, "The fact that in your report you state that the ILA shares your decision on the West Village is untrue. I say firmly that we are against the West Village project." [81]

Alex Dobkin, an artist member of CSWV, checked with

Artists' Equity Association. Although Elias Newman, president of the New York chapter, had testified in favor of the plan, no vote had been taken in the Association. On November 21, the board of directors of Artists' Equity met and voted to oppose any project in the West Village and also any designation of the area as blighted.[82] Erik Wensberg spoke to Harry Van Arsdale, Jr., president of the Central Labor Council, and got him to over-rule the testimony that had been given CPC by the chairman of the Council's housing committee. The Council "is neither for nor against the project," said Van Arsdale.[83]

With a large part of his interest-group support gone and with the Mayor riding high on the momentum of his election victory, Felt had few defenses left. Early in January, Felt met with Hortense Gabel, the Mayor's consultant on housing, Julius Edelstein, the Mayor's special assistant, and Jack Lutsky, the Mayor's counsel. The three of them, particularly Edelstein, ap-plied persuasion and pressure to get Felt to remove the designa-tion. Finally they succeeded. On January 12, Wagner wrote Felt, saying that "the time has come to put the West Village proposal to rest." Felt replied three days later, agreeing and say-ing that steps to remove the designation would be undertaken immediately.[84] On January 31, CPC met and unanimously adopted the removal of the designation. The West Villagers had triumphed.

AFTER THE BATTLE

On February 25, 1962, CSWV held a meeting to consider its future.[85] It decided to change the name of the organization to the West Village Committee (WVC) and to hold annual elec-tions for a chairman and four other officers. "A large executive committee" was to be appointed by the officers. A list of twenty committees, with activities ranging from "businessmen's informa-tion" to "experimental housing" was drawn up. It was decided that "nothing will be done without the consensus of the neighborhood" and that "nothing will be done that hurts any resident." The WVC's newsletter proclaimed, "The work to save the West Village is finished, and work to improve the West Village is begun. Long live the West Village." [86]

Work to improve the West Village was begun. A new slate of officers, with Hugh Byfield as chairman, was elected. Members went to work on the various committees, and proposals for a community center and for experimental housing were formulated. On May 5, 1963, the committee held a press conference at which it made public plans for construction of 475 apartments in a series of five-story structures in the West Village area. The plans for the buildings were said to be a new concept in urban housing.[87] WVC applied to the city for Mitchell-Lama funds to finance construction of the apartments, but the city has not yet given its approval for the grant. The West Villagers blame CPC for the delay in approving the funds.[88]

Members of the committee did not confine themselves to the West Village. Mrs. Jacobs and others gave aid and advice to the residents of the Cobble Hill section of Brooklyn on how to combat an urban renewal project that had been proposed for that area. They also advised the people of Tompkins Square on how to fight the city. WVC spent much time combatting the proposed Lower Manhattan expressway, and Mrs. Jacobs and several other West Villagers testified at the public hearings. The expressway was voted down by the Board of Estimate, although the proposal was later revived and is now again being considered by the city government.

It was not long before "the enemy" was perceived to be again threatening the West Village. The first postvictory newsletter of WVC had been full of optimism and constructive suggestions, but the second issue, which came out in April, was headed, "New Threat!" [89] The new threat was the Board of Estimate's order for a preliminary study of a proposal to build an elevated

truck route to Washington Street where an old railroad spur
was being torn down. WVC wrote to the Mayor and met with
the Borough President and other officials, and the study was put
off.

Toward the end of May city Traffic Commissioner Henry
Barnes announced that he intended to change the flow of traffic
on Greenwich Street from one way northbound to one way
southbound and to change the bus routes in the area. WVC
stated that the proposed changes would make Greenwich Street
a through truck route, would place an overload of traffic on
Greenwich Street, and, worst of all, might lead to the widening
of the street. On June 2 WVC went to court to seek a permanent injunction against the changes. In July the court ruled
against the Villagers and in favor of Barnes, but as of December,
1963, the changes had still not been put into effect.

Neither of these later "threats" to the West Village succeeded
in creating the same *esprit* that had been achieved during the
urban renewal fight. The cohesiveness that had prevailed
throughout the major battle began to wear off. WVC, which
had always consisted primarily of middle-class professionals, increasingly lost contact with the Irish and Puerto Rican segments
of the neighborhood.

WVC also fell prey to internal dissension. Some of the important members, like Zoll, had been attracted largely by the excitement of the fight. When WVC made several decisions with
which he did not agree, Zoll lost interest in its work. Byfield, the
first postvictory chairman of the committee, became so embit-
tered with the internal politics of the organization that he
severed all connections with it.

If WVC lost some of its leading officials, the city government
did also. On January 20, 1962, Davies, the chairman of HRB,
submitted his resignation, primarily because of business commit-
ments, although the battle over West Village had probably increased his desire to leave city service. A year later Felt resigned

as chairman of CPC, although he continued to serve as a member. His defeat over West Village was one of several factors that contributed to his decision to step down.

The community renewal study of the entire Greenwich Village area, which CPC had intended to undertake at the same time as the West Village project, was started but then abandoned. It seems clear that the city government, or at least the departments concerned with housing and planning, have no desire to run the risk of another battle with the Villagers. If improved housing conditions are achieved, it will not be through urban renewal. Some high-rent apartment houses may be built by private investors, although new zoning regulations in the area have put a damper on this type of construction. It remains to be seen whether the positive programs of the West Villagers will be put into execution, and, if they are, what their effect on the community will be.

CHAPTER V

The West Side Urban Renewal Area

THE WEST SIDE

The area of Manhattan Island lying between Central Park and the Hudson River and between 59th and 110th Streets has been officially named by the City Planning Commission "Park West." It is known to most residents of the city, however, by the less precise name, "The West Side." The area was once one of the most fashionable parts of the city, but in the past thirty years it has declined sharply. "The East Side," particularly between 59th and 96th Street, is now the place where most of New York's high-income families make their homes.

The development of the West Side as a concentrated residential area began in 1880.[1] In that year the elevated railroad, powered by steam locomotives, was built along Columbus Avenue. It put the West Side just a few minutes away from the downtown business and shopping centers. The construction of the "El" resulted almost immediately in a building boom. Along and near Central Park luxurious mansions of marble and brick were built. In the side streets came the brownstones, three to five stories high, inhabited by middle-class families and those upper-class families who could not afford a mansion. Along Columbus Avenue, beneath the noise and soot of the trains, along part of Amsterdam Avenue, and in some of the side streets between Amsterdam and Columbus were built the notorious tenements, housing the poorer members of the community.

Between 1901 and 1930 the boom on the West Side continued. Riverside Drive was opened in 1900. Shortly thereafter the "El" was electrified, and in 1904 the Broadway subway line was completed. Between 1910 and 1930 a large number of tall apartment houses were built along Broadway, West End Avenue, Riverside Drive, Central Park West, and the wider side streets. The buildings constructed during this period still provide most of the good housing in the West Side.

With the advent of the Depression, new construction on the West Side ceased almost completely. The opening of the Eighth Avenue subway along Central Park West in 1932 produced no immediate effect; the removal of the "El" tracks from Columbus Avenue in 1941 similarly attracted slight interest.

Following World War II, construction on the West Side did not resume. Instead of new building, many of the older structures, particularly the brownstones, were converted into rooming houses. At the same time the composition of the population in the area began to change. Up to this time the higher income areas had been inhabited mostly by Jews, while along Columbus and Amsterdam Avenues and in the side streets the population was largely of Irish extraction. Following World War II, and particularly after 1950, the Irish began to move out, and their place was taken by a large number of Puerto Ricans and some Negroes.

These changes can best be illustrated by some of CPC's figures for the area that was eventually picked for urban renewal. This area was bounded by 87th and 97th Streets and by Central Park West and Amsterdam Avenue (see Figure 3). Of the 33,000 persons living in these blocks in 1950, 1.3 percent were nonwhite, 4.9 percent were Puerto Rican, and 93.8 percent were white (other than Puerto Rican). By 1956 the population of the area had increased to 39,000, of which 9.1 percent were nonwhite, 33.4 percent were Puerto Rican, and only 57.5 percent were white.[2] The 6,000 increase in population was accommodated mainly through subdivision of larger apartments

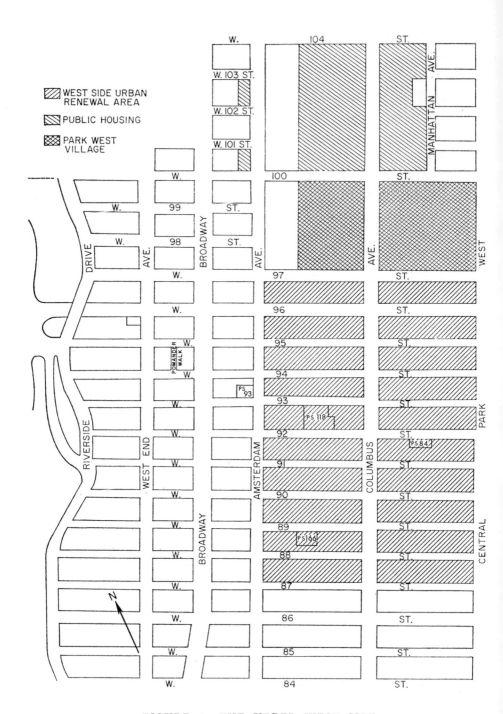

FIGURE 3. THE UPPER WEST SIDE

and through conversion of furnished rooms into regular dwelling units by the addition of minimum housekeeping equipment. In 1956 almost 20 percent of all living quarters in the area were overcrowded, and one-third were without adequate bathroom facilities.[3]

Certain actions of the city government accelerated the decline of the area. In 1952, SCC turned over to a group of sponsors the area between 97th and 100th Streets from Central Park West to Amsterdam Avenue for development as a Title I project to be known as Manhattantown.[4] Over 4,000 dwelling units were torn down,[5] and the majority of those relocated could not afford the rents in the new project. Many of these people moved into the area south of the site, thus increasing the overcrowded conditions that already existed. Meanwhile, the project, which was the first urban renewal in the area, became a symbol of corruption, callousness, and prejudice to many of the residents of the West Side. This attitude toward urban renewal was reinforced a few years later by the Columbus Circle and Lincoln Square projects. Both projects were located near the southern boundary of the Park West community. Both involved extensive relocation, particularly of Puerto Ricans, and in both cases the new construction was primarily nonresidential. The small amount of residential construction that did take place consisted of apartments that were too expensive for those who had previously lived on the site.

Once the deterioration of the West Side area had begun and cheap housing could be found, the Department of Welfare began to place some of its clientele in the rooming houses and converted dwellings. This increased the number of problem families in the area and hastened its decline. By 1956 the West Side contained some of the worst housing in the city.

Despite the deterioration of the area, the West Side still contained a large number of people with leadership ability. Along

Central Park West and Riverside Drive remained many families who had moved in when the apartment buildings were new and fashionable. Along West End Avenue and in some of the side streets, large apartments at comparatively low rentals could still be found. Many young professionals moved into these apartments, some probably awaiting the time when they could afford to move to the East Side, some finding the West Side a better place to live and bring up children.

The resources of this leadership group were tapped by the large number of organizations in the community. There were many churches and synagogues, representing almost every denomination. In some streets block associations had been formed to plant trees, fix up buildings, and keep the street clean. Many women in the area were involved with the local settlement houses or with the P-TA.

The number of organizations in the community is illustrated by the fact that the local council formed to represent the twenty-block renewal area contained more than forty separate organizations. Perhaps because of the large number of organizations and the economic and ethnic heterogeneity of the population, there is no single dominant organization on the West Side. The strongest organizations are probably the Democratic Party Reform clubs, which have succeeded in attracting many of the liberal middle-class members of the population. The reformers' strength is indicated by the fact that between 1951 and 1961 they succeeded in capturing all the assembly districts on the upper West Side.

The Reform clubs differ from the regular clubs in their general political orientation and in their internal organization. They are far more concerned with substantive issues of policy. On the local scene, the issue that was usually of most concern to the Reformers, aside from the reform of the Party, was housing. The Reform clubs conducted rent clinics, inspected houses for code violations, and took an active interest in the city's housing and planning policies. The major internal difference between the Reform clubs and the regular clubs is that in the latter, power is centralized in the district leader, whereas in the Reform clubs, power is dispersed among a larger number of individuals. This dispersion of power has been given institutional form through an elaborate system of committees, and thus any member may exercise his talents and play an active role within a committee. In most of the Reform clubs the housing committee was one of the most important, and the chairmanship of it sometimes served as a stepping-stone to higher office or even the district leadership.[6]

The FDR–Woodrow Wilson Democrats, the club in the same Assembly District as the urban renewal area, began in 1959 as an amalgamation of three existing clubs that had been competing for power within the District. Ever since its formation, the club has been known for its militancy in the cause of the Reform and also for its internal disunity.[7] Wilson quotes one of the club leaders as saying, "We have been in a constant state of turmoil since our very inception. . . . There's no general agreement on leadership." [8] This internal conflict was to reveal itself in the club's efforts to take a stand on the urban renewal plan.

The influx of Puerto Ricans during the 1950s had little effect on the Reform clubs or on the other West Side organizations. The Puerto Ricans showed little interest in joining any of the existing organizations, and they did not organize themselves on a neighborhood basis. The organizations that they did form tended to fall into two categories. A number of "home-town clubs" were formed whose membership consisted of those who had come from the same town or city in Puerto Rico. These groups limited themselves to purely social functions. In the second category were a number of citywide organizations. These groups tended to shy away from political activity except in so far as such activity furthered the careers of their leaders. None of the citywide Puerto Rican organizations had a high degree of grass-roots support. The language barrier and the newcomers' lack of familiarity with American urban life resulted in a dearth of both leaders and members.

The most powerful Puerto Rican organization in New York is not a private group but an official agency of the Puerto Rican government. This is the New York City Office of the Commonwealth of Puerto Rico. The Commonwealth Office was originally established to find jobs for Puerto Rican immigrants. As its staff and its influence grew, it gradually expanded its interests to cover almost all activities of the New York Puerto Rican community. The private Puerto Rican groups were overshadowed by the prestige and the resources of the Commonwealth Office. Up until the West Side controversy, however, the Office had not taken any action in the field of housing.

The controversy over the West Side Urban Renewal Area (WSURA) produced a few Puerto Rican leaders and dramatized the plight of the Puerto Rican community. Many other West Side groups were affected by events related to the urban renewal project, events that began in 1955.

THE URBAN RENEWAL AREA

The Conception of the Project. As will be recalled from Chapter II, in 1954 Congress passed a new National Housing Act containing provisions for federal support of renewal projects that combined conservation and rehabilitation with new construction. Mayor Wagner and other members of the city administration wanted to utilize the new provisions of this act, but they were hampered by the opposition of Moses, whose SCC had responsibility for all urban renewal. Moses was a strong advocate of total clearance and was convinced that rehabilitation and conservation would not help to clear slums.

On October 5, 1955, Mayor Wagner was scheduled to appear before the Housing Subcommittee of the House Banking and Currency Committee to testify on appropriations for urban renewal. The Mayor was looking for something spectacular that he could include in his testimony. The answer to his problem came, a few weeks before his scheduled appearance, from Samuel Ratensky, the Planning Director for the New York City Housing Authority.

Ratensky had himself been looking for an apartment on the upper West Side and had been impressed by how much the area had declined in the past few years. Knowing that many of the buildings were still structurally sound, it occurred to him that the West Side would be an ideal place to try out the provisions of the 1954 Housing Act. He broached the idea to Philip Cruise of the State Housing Commission and to Warren Moscow of the Housing Authority. They reacted favorably.

Ratensky, accompanied by Cruise and Moscow, then went to see the Mayor. They urged him to announce to the congressional subcommittee that the more than 200 blocks between 59th and 125th Streets and between Central and Morningside Parks and the Hudson River would be declared an urban renewal area. The vast scope of the project would show dramatically the uses to which conservation and rehabilitation could be put. They convinced Wagner to use the plan, and on October 5 he presented the idea to the subcommittee. Moses had not been informed of the plan, nor had he been consulted about the Mayor's testimony.

Once the proposal became public, it was subjected to the differing viewpoints and criticisms of the people and agencies who would have to administer it. A series of discussions took place attended by representatives of the CPC, SCC, the Housing Authority, the Department of Buildings, the State Division of Housing, and the Borough President of Manhattan. There was talk of cutting the project down to four or six blocks.[9] It was finally decided, with Ratensky's concurrence, to undertake a pilot rehabilitation study of the twenty-block area from 87th to 97th Streets between Central Park West and Amsterdam Avenue (Figure 3).

On February 24, 1956, the Board of Estimate approved a request by the city for $150,000 of federal funds to finance a study of the area. The city was to provide an additional $75,000. In May the federal government provided the money under the Urban Renewal Administration's Demonstration Grant Program. In June, CPC declared the area as "deteriorating" to pave the way for acceptance of the grant.

The firm of Brown and Guenther, architectural consultants, was named to undertake the study. A large number of planners, economists, architects, and community relations experts were appointed to assist in the analysis of the area and to formulate proposals for renewal. In the summer of 1956, research work in the West Side began. From the beginning there was an emphasis on community cooperation. A questionnaire asking each resident what he would like a new apartment to include was distributed. The city planners were quoted as saying that any rehabilitation program would fail without citizen participation.[10]

Work on the study continued throughout 1957. Finally, in April, 1958, the report was completed and released to the public in a 96-page elaborately illustrated brochure.[11] The brochure contained two alternative plans, one emphasizing rehabilitation, the other emphasizing new construction. Each plan was divided into four stages, each stage to last for two and a half years. Both plans involved a minimum of public subsidies because "what is proposed for the Study Area must be of such a nature that it can be repeated again and again in the constant modernization and reconstruction which must take place in every city." [12] Somewhere between 2,161 and 2,394 dwelling units, depending on which plan and what kind of financing was used, were to be rehabilitated or constructed in the first and second stages. Of this number 474 were to be low-income public housing. The brochure also contained a brief section setting forth a proposed scheme for community participation in the planning and execution of the project.

The initial reaction to the Brown and Guenther report was

favorable both in the site area and in the city as a whole. Individuals and groups active in the housing field hailed the proposals as a bold new departure in the concept of urban renewal. The favorable reaction of the site residents "was based largely on the conception that the plan would involve essentially rehabilitation; would be flexible (the alternative plans proposed in the study period); would involve little displacement of residents, and was 'different' from the 'bulldozing' approach." [13]

It was clear that Moses, who was hostile to the whole plan, would not be its administrator. Thus, in May, 1958, the Mayor established the Urban Renewal Board, whose prime function was to implement the recommendations contained in the Brown and Guenther report. James Felt, chairman of CPC, was named to head the Board. The other members were the City Budget Director, the Corporation Counsel, the Buildings Commissioner, the Director of the Bureau of Real Estate, the Chairman of the New York City Housing Authority, and the chief engineer of the Board of Estimate. Ratensky was given a leave of absence from the Housing Authority and was named executive director of the Board.

Felt, after much bargaining, got Moses to agree to allow the Urban Renewal Board to have priority in using the federal funds available for New York. In September, 1958, it was announced that HHFA would set aside $4 million for the first year of the project. In December, the federal government advanced the city $400,000 for project planning.

During its first year the Urban Renewal Board worked on formulating a detailed plan for the twenty-block area. It also intended to carry out a "brick-and-mortar" pilot project in the area, taking a few brownstones on one block and demonstrating various ways in which they could be rehabilitated. This idea got bogged down, however, in numerous legal questions and was also delayed because of FHA's inexperience in processing such demonstration projects.

In January, 1959, Felt announced that a number of qualified sponsors were ready to bid on various parts of the project. Later in the month the City Housing Authority submitted to CPC blueprints for a 400-apartment low-cost project located between 90th and 91st Streets. In May, 1959, the preliminary plan was finally ready. Its public announcement stirred the site residents into activity.

The Opposition Forms. The Brown and Guenther report had envisioned a three-level program of citizen participation in connection with the West Side project. The first level would consist of the groups in the site area, which would be aided by a community organization worker, the second level would consist of the organizations in the entire Park West community, and finally there would be a consultant group, made up of key city-wide organizations, which would advise the city agencies on the whole urban renewal program.[14]

Prior to the announcement of the preliminary plan, the Urban Renewal Board attempted to organize the citywide consultant group. A chairman could not be found, however, and there was some disagreement as to what groups should be represented. It was finally decided to put this part of the program in abeyance.

The effort to set up a group representing the whole West Side community was more successful. A nucleus of prominent West Side citizens under the leadership of Stanley Lowell, who had just resigned as Deputy Mayor, had already met to discuss urban renewal. Elizabeth Kempton, the community organization specialist for the Urban Renewal Board, and representatives of the Community Council of Greater New York met with Lowell's group to select the membership of what was to be the Park to Hudson Urban Renewal Citizens' Committee.

The Community Council had been chosen to sponsor the citizen participation program so that the program would qualify for grants from private foundations. The Council was given the job of selecting and supervising the social workers who were to implement the citizen participation program. The Citizens' Housing and Planning Council was also chosen as a sponsor. United Neighborhood Houses, which had been the organization most concerned with the initial planning of citizen participation, was annoyed at not having been selected to sponsor the program and made no attempt to hide its indignation.

On January 26, 1959, Mayor Wagner officially announced the formation of Park-Hudson. Stanley Lowell was made chairman, and thirty individuals were listed as members. A grant of $36,000 had been obtained from the Lavanburg Foundation. John J. Foley, a professional community organizer, was hired to be executive director, and an office and a full-time secretary were also acquired. The Mayor's announcement also contained the statement, "Organization of a citizen participation program within the twenty block project area will get underway immediately, and as soon as a representative group is formed there, it will have membership on the Park-Hudson Committee." [15] The apparent contradiction between this statement and the three separate levels envisioned in the Brown and Guenther report was later to cause much confusion.

The publication of the preliminary plan came as something of a shock to the site area. The plan set forth in concrete detail the general ideas which had been contained in the Brown and Guenther report of the year before. It called for the construction of 7,800 new housing units—400 of them low-income, 2,400 middle-income, and the remaining 5,000 units to be high-income. Both sides of Columbus Avenue were to be torn down to permit widening of the avenue, 4,300 families and an additional 1,500 single persons were to be relocated to make way for new construction, and an unspecified number of people would also have to be moved to permit rehabilitation work on the brownstones. The large number of small businesses located along Columbus Avenue would all have to be relocated.

As the individuals who would be affected by the plan realized

its potential impact, they were galvanized into action. The first
to organize were the businessmen of the area. Several days after
the announcement of the plan, Dr. Thomas Matthew, a Negro
neurosurgeon living on Central Park West, formed the West
Side Business and Professional Group. It was formed for the
specific purpose of combatting the plan. Within two months
about 100 of the 461 shopowners in the area had joined the
group.[16]

The businessmen also helped to set up a tenants' committee.
On June 25 about 150 people led by Jane Wahlberg, a social
worker, met to organize the West Side Tenants Committee. The
Committee took the stand that the plan did not meet the needs
of the site residents and that there should be more low- and
middle-income housing and less relocation. The Tenants Committee established a joint headquarters with the Business and Professional Group in a store on West 96th Street.[17]

The pastors of the two Catholic churches in the area, St.
Gregory's and Holy Name, also came out against the plan.
Their parishioners consisted mostly of the old Irish inhabitants
of the area along with a growing number of Puerto Ricans.
These two groups would be hard hit by the proposed renewal,
and the pastors feared that a substantial portion of their parishioners who would not be able to afford the high-income housing
would have to move to other parts of the city.

The Tenants Committee was short-lived, but the businessmen
and the churches had another potential ally in the area's Puerto
Rican population. The Puerto Ricans lacked organization, however, and it was to be a while before they made their voices
heard.

The city took measures to combat the opposition. During
May and June, over thirty public meetings were held at which
public officials explained the contents of the plan. Foley, of the
Community Council staff, met with all the organizations and in-

stitutions in the area to explain the plan and determine the community's reaction to it.[18]

On June 29 CPC held its public hearing on the preliminary plan. Thirty-six speakers appeared, most of them favoring the plan generally. There was, however, widespread agreement that the amount of low- and middle-income housing should be increased and that there should be more compensation for businessmen who had to be relocated. On July 15 CPC issued its report. It approved the preliminary plan but increased the number of low-income units by 200 and the number of middle-income units by 1,200. The "mix" of low, middle, and high-income housing was thus changed from 400–2,400–5,000 to 600–3,600–3,600. CPC also promised to do what it could to relieve the burden imposed on the small businessmen.

CPC's modifications did little to appease the opposition in the site area. Opponents of the plan increased their drive to gain community support and began attempts to coordinate their efforts.[19] At the same time, however, events were taking place that would markedly change the actions of the site residents.

The Brown and Guenther report had envisioned an independent neighborhood organization representing the twenty-block site area. The proposal submitted to the Lavanburg Foundation, on which basis the money for a professional community organization staff had been obtained, seemed to indicate the same:

A method must be developed to bring the people in the twenty-block area designated for renewal into effective participation with the official agency in the renewal program. . . . A neighborhood organization, representative of the various interests involved . . . is required.[20]

Since the site residents had not yet been organized, in the early summer of 1959, Foley hired an additional community organizer, Michael Coffey. Coffey, acting with the knowledge and consent of Foley and Miss Kempton, set about laying the groundwork for an independent council of groups within the site area. By the beginning of August a Provisional Council of Organizations in the West Side Urban Renewal Area was established. Milton Akers, director of the Walden School, was named Provisional President. Seventeen organizations were represented on the Council, and many others had expressed interest in joining.[21] The Council emphatically asserted its independence from Park-Hudson.

When Lowell, the chairman of the Park-Hudson Committee, heard about the formation of the Provisional Council, he was shocked. He had not been informed of Coffey's activities, and he felt that he was a victim of sabotage by a member of his own staff. It had been his understanding that any organization representing the site would be incorporated into Park-Hudson, as had been stated in the Mayor's press release announcing the formation of Park-Hudson.

The misunderstanding about the status of the Provisional Council was compounded by general confusion as to who was really responsible for the activities of the professional staff. Coffey and Foley considered themselves under the supervision of the executive director of the Community Council, who had the power to hire and fire them. Mrs. Randolph Guggenheimer, the chairman of the Community Council's Neighborhood and Regional Planning Board and the Council's representative on Park-Hudson, believed that the staff should report to her. Lowell assumed that the staff was working for him. This confusion was never resolved, but, regardless of who was in charge, the Provisional Council had been firmly established and was destined to grow in strength.

Over the summer of 1959 the preliminary plan became involved with the internal struggles of the city's Democratic Party. The city's primary elections were scheduled for September 15. The Fifth Assembly District North, in which the site area was located, was the scene of a battle between the regular and reform factions of the Party. Dennis Mahon, a former Borough President of Manhattan and a regular, was the district leader. Irving Wolfson, the head of the FDR–Woodrow Wilson Democrats, a Reform club, was attempting to unseat Mahon and gain control of the district for the Reformers. The Board of Estimate did not wish to decide on the West Side plan while the leadership of the area was in dispute, and thus, late in June, on the motion of Manhattan Borough President Hulan Jack, the Board of Estimate voted not to consider the preliminary plan until September 17, two days after the primary.

The primary election also posed a problem for the Provisional Council. Both Wolfson and Mahon wanted their clubs to be represented on the Council, but Wolfson objected strongly to Mahon being represented and Mahon objected strongly to Wolfson being represented. Foley negotiated with both sides and worked out a compromise solution whereby neither club would be officially a member of the Council but both could send representatives who would be permitted to speak at Council meetings.

On September 11, Felt announced that the project would be divided into three sections so that the maximum number of families and businesses could be relocated within the area. He also emphasized the statement made in the preliminary plan that the city, rather than a private developer, would handle the relocation work. This proposed procedure for relocation was a departure from the city's practice in other urban renewal projects, where the developer had given the relocation work to a private company.

On September 15 Wolfson beat Mahon in the primary election. On September 17 the Board of Estimate held its public hearing on the preliminary plan. Twenty-three speakers generally favored the plan, and seventeen went on record as generally opposed. The Board set October 22 as the date when it would announce its decision.

The opinion of Hulan Jack, since he represented the borough in which the project was located, carried special weight with the Board of Estimate. Jack had been approached by representatives of the Provisional Council and had placed the services of his executive assistant, Tom Lawless, at the disposal of the Council. Several meetings had taken place in which Jack had listened to the grievances and suggestions of organizations from the site area. On October 20 Jack announced that he favored the preliminary plan in principle, but that he wanted to increase the number of low-income units to 1,000 and the number of middle-income units to 4,200. On October 22, 1959, the Board met, made the changes Jack had suggested, and then unanimously approved the preliminary plan. The battle over the final plan remained to be fought.

Park-Hudson and Stryckers Bay. Up to the time of the September, 1959, Board of Estimate hearing on the preliminary plan, the Provisional Council avoided the question of whether it was to become a permanent formal organization. By October, however, it was clear to all members that the creation of a formal organization was a logical and necessary step. In November the group held a "constitutional convention," and on December 16 it was formally rechristened as the Stryckers Bay Neighborhood Council.

Akers, who had been the provisional president, was elected to continue as head of Stryckers Bay. Akers was sophisticated and was skillful at handling meetings, but his greatest virtue was his extraordinary neutrality. No one could figure out where he stood on most of the major issues facing the council.

Stryckers Bay Neighborhood Council was composed of two delegates from each member group. Eventually the membership of the Council reached a total of forty-three groups—ten churches and synagogues, eight schools, eight block associations, six political clubs, five P-TA's, two Puerto Rican groups, and four other organizations. The delegates from almost all the organizations were completely free to vote as they wished, even in cases where the organization they represented had already taken a stand on the issue under debate.

The constitution of the Council called for an executive committee that was to be a working group unhindered by the need to represent the various interests in the area. A twelve-man advisory committee was to be set up with members nominated by each of the major interests. The advisory committee was to have the power to veto decisions of the executive committee. This advisory committee arrangement was never put into operation, because some of the interest groups that had to meet to settle on a single member—the four Jewish organizations, for example— could never reach sufficient agreement to decide on one person to represent them. Thus, the contest for power in the organization centered on the executive committee and the officers. The first slate elected had three vice-presidents under Akers—Dr. Matthew of the Business and Professional Group, the Reverend Henry J. Browne of St. Gregory's Catholic Church, and Aramis Gomez representing the Puerto Ricans.

The businessmen did not stay in the Council very long. The Puerto Rican businessmen in the area refused to join any organization, and the remaining businessmen, organized as the 87th- 97th Street Business and Professional Group, lacked any degree of unity. The individual members were primarily concerned with their own individual futures and were continually trying to make side deals concerning relocation sites, stores in the new projects, and so forth. Early in 1960 the business group jettisoned Dr. Matthew. That he was not a businessman caused some resentment. The main problem, however, was that the members simply wanted to use the group to express their unhappiness with urban renewal, whereas Dr. Matthew tried to formulate plans and compromises that would alleviate the plight of the whole business community. The two conceptions of the group's purposes proved incompatible.

Dr. Matthew was succeeded by Sylvia Wollan. She found herself constantly opposing majority decisions of Stryckers Bay. The Stryckers Bay leaders found that she was constantly blocking positive action and that she tended to monopolize conversation during the Council's meetings with city officials. Early in the spring of 1960, when the Stryckers Bay executive committee chose representatives to the city's Relocation Advisory Committee, it named several business people but ignored Mrs. Wollan. She then managed to withdraw the business group from the Council, stating that Stryckers Bay no longer represented the businessmen's interests.[22]

Representation of the Puerto Ricans on Stryckers Bay also presented a problem. Although there were a number of citywide Puerto Rican organizations, there were no West Side organizations representing the Puerto Rican population, and none of the citywide organizations were concerned with housing or urban renewal. The leadership of the Puerto Ricans in WSURA thus fell to two individuals, Aramis Gomez and Efrain Rosa.

Gomez and Rosa were an effective team. Gomez was a fine public speaker, sharp-witted and humorous. Rosa was quiet and diplomatic—far more inclined to negotiate than was Gomez. As Gomez himself stated, he would do the yelling while Rosa would do the compromising. Gomez had first become involved with urban renewal when he found himself about to be evicted to make way for the Lincoln Square project. He had believed that the city government could do no wrong, but some of the people opposing the Lincoln Square project showed him the Manhattantown site and thus convinced him that something was amiss with the city's housing policies. He has remained an opponent of these policies ever since. Rosa had been active in several city-wide Puerto Rican organizations, and when Gomez became active in the renewal controversy, Rosa followed his lead.

Because Stryckers Bay was hard-put to find organizations to represent Puerto Ricans, Rosa and Gomez were each seated as a separate delegation. Rosa represented the Spanish-American Cultural Association, a citywide group; Gomez sat as the head of the Spanish-American Committee of WSURA. Coffey, aided by Joseph Morales of the Office of the Commonwelath of Puerto Rico, tried to make Gomez' committee into an organization that would truly represent the West Side Puerto Ricans. The attempt was unsuccessful, however, and the committee remained a letterhead organization whose sole purpose was to give Gomez a voice in Stryckers Bay. Neither Rosa nor Gomez wanted to be hampered by an organization.

As the Stryckers Bay Neighborhood Council solidified its organization and gained increasing strength in the renewal area, it more and more sapped the strength of the Park-Hudson Committee. The enmity between the two groups was mutual. Lowell disliked the Council because it had been formed behind his back and because he could see in it an obvious threat to the existence of his own committee. The people in Stryckers Bay disliked Park-Hudson because they considered it an unrepresentative group, strongly weighted in favor of the plan, which presumed to speak for their area. They resented the lack of contact between Park-Hudson and the site area. Wolfson, the District Leader of the Fifth A.D. North, complained that the only way he could find out what Park-Hudson was doing was by having spies within the committee.

The leaders of Stryckers Bay along with the leaders of the FDR–Woodrow Wilson Democrats set about pursuing a deliberate strategy to cause the collapse of Park-Hudson. The strategy was based on the concept of neighborhood representation. Stryckers Bay demanded that the city keep its promise to heed the wishes of the site area and declared that Stryckers Bay, not Park-Hudson, was the voice of the neighborhood. When the city decided to establish a Relocation Advisory Committee for the renewal area, it called upon Park-Hudson to name seven representatives and for Stryckers Bay to name an equal number.

Stryckers Bay refused, militantly insisting that it be given a majority voice. The dispute was finally resolved by appointment of the three members of Park-Hudson who were also members of Stryckers Bay as delegates from Park-Hudson. The final composition of the committee thus consisted of four members of Park-Hudson, seven members of Stryckers Bay, and three individuals who were members of both organizations. Despite this ingenious compromise, the disunity within the advisory committee was so great that it collapsed.[23]

At the same time that the conflict between Stryckers Bay and Park-Hudson was being waged, there was also some friction between Stryckers Bay and the FDR–Woodrow Wilson Democrats. These were now the two most important organizations in the area, and with the entire future of the area at stake, each was anxious to have as large a voice as possible in influencing the city's course of action. Most of the conflict between the club and the Council came over issues of publicity. Each accused the other of trying to monopolize the mass media and of not giving proper credit for work the other group had done. Some people also accused FDR–Woodrow Wilson of trying to dominate Stryckers Bay by infiltrating the various delegations to the Council. There was some overlapping membership, but this was not the result of any deliberate plan. Several of the representatives of the synagogues, the settlement houses, and the P-TA's were members of the Reform club, but the overlapping membership was never so great as to give FDR–Woodrow Wilson a dominant voice in Stryckers Bay. Most of the activists in the political club were unaware that the club had any contact with Stryckers Bay.[24]

At the January 11, 1960, meeting of the Park-Hudson Steering Committee, Lowell moved that Park-Hudson should vote itself out of existence because of the apparent reluctance of Stryckers Bay to cooperate. The move was voted down, but the meetings of Park-Hudson became increasingly less frequent.

Finally, in September, 1960, Lowell resigned. He was succeeded by Charles Ascher, a professor of political science at Brooklyn College who was active in civic affairs. Park-Hudson continued its efforts to obtain code-enforcement in the blocks peripheral to the renewal area, and it showed interest in cooperating in the formulation of neighborhood renewal plans for areas north and south of the site.[25] In April, 1961, however, HRB informed Park-Hudson that it would no longer provide the Committee with money for a staff but would simply provide staff services from HRB's own personnel when needed. The meetings of the Committee grew still less frequent, and it finally died quietly, the victim of Stryckers Bay.

While Stryckers Bay was gaining a firm foothold in the site area, the city continued the long process of moving toward final approval for the project. So many parts of the proposed plan were novel ideas that had never been tried before that much delay was encountered at the state and federal as well as at the local levels of government.

In February, 1960, the city announced that it was reviving the demonstration project. Twenty brownstones were to be converted to discover the costs and proper methods of carrying out such rehabilitation. Approval was received from the Board of Estimate and the federal government, and in the fall work began.

In June, 1960, the newly organized HRB took over jurisdiction of WSURA from the Urban Renewal Board. This did not involve any discontinuity in personnel. Davies, the chairman of HRB, had been vice-chairman of the Urban Renewal Board in his former capacity as Commissioner of Real Estate. He had worked, and continued to work, in the closest possible cooperation with Planning Commissioner Felt. Ratensky, the executive director of the Urban Renewal Board, became head of project planning for HRB.

In December HRB submitted its relocation plan for the West

Side to the Board of Estimate. The relocation plan represented a reversal of policy, for instead of the city establishing a central agency to handle all the relocation work, as had been promised in the preliminary plan, relocation was to be carried out by private firms hired by the individual project sponsors, as had been the practice in the past. The reason for this reversal was to be found in the two reports prepared for the Mayor by J. Anthony Panuch, who had been hired by the city as Special Adviser on Housing and Urban Renewal. Panuch's first report, issued in December, 1959, dealt with relocation.[26] The second, issued on March, 1960, dealt with the administrative organization of housing and urban renewal in New York.[27] HRB had been established in accordance with the second report, and it felt bound to follow Panuch's recommendations. In the relocation report Panuch had flatly rejected the idea of a central relocation bureau. Thus, HRB reversed the stand the Urban Renewal Board had taken. This policy led to charges by some neighborhood groups that the city's promises were no good, and many of the groups in the area insisted to the very end that the city should do the relocation work.

On January 6, 1961, Mayor Wagner announced the sponsors for fifteen projects in the first stage of the renewal plan. He stated that construction in the first stage would begin in April or May. Various obstacles, however, were destined to delay the beginning of work for considerably longer.

The Opposition Hardens. As the time drew near for CPC and the Board of Estimate to pass judgment on a final plan, activity among the organizations on the West Side increased markedly. The three major groups in the site area—the Puerto Ricans, the FDR–Woodrow Wilson Democrats, and Stryckers Bay—mobilized their forces and crystallized their final attitudes toward the project.

On July 13, 1961, a group of Puerto Rican leaders held an emergency meeting to consider the effect of the city's housing program, the West Side project in particular, on the Puerto

Rican community. The outcome of the meeting was the formation of the Puerto Rican Citizens' Housing Committee. The Committee had only five members—Roland Cintron, Aramis Gomez, Josephine Nieves, Efrain Rosa, and Petra Rosa. Miss Nieves, Mrs. Rosa, and Cintron had each received some training in social work or community organization and had worked for various city agencies concerned with the Puerto Rican population. The Committee soon obtained that prime ingredient of organizational success, a staff. COIR, which had been partly responsible for the Committee's formation, provided a staff worker. The Office of the Commonwealth of Puerto Rico gave the Committee a place to meet and also assigned one of its community organizers, Roberto Casablanca, to work with the Committee.

The members of the Committee were not newcomers to the field of housing, and they had formed very definite opinions about the city's housing and renewal programs. They later stated that at the time of the formation of the Citizens' Housing Committee they believed

1. That the Puerto Ricans were being "pushed" out of so-called prime real estate in Manhattan. 2. That the Puerto Rican community was being ignored on the planning and execution of any housing program. 3. That the relocation program as presently administered is working to the detriment of the Puerto Rican community, and, finally, 4. That the overall housing program seems to envision a New York without Puerto Ricans.[28]

In January, 1962, the Committee issued a report that was widely distributed. It recommended a minimum of bulldozing and relocation and a maximum of low-income housing. It stated that at least 30 percent of the proposed housing in the WSURA should be low-income. It doubted the sincerity of the city's efforts at citizen participation:

One classic example of questionable community participation is the West Side Urban Renewal Area where the community was supposedly organized on the basis of neighborhood organizations. Of the forty organizations that represent the neighborhood only two are Puerto Rican. Is this equitable representation when the majority of the residents are Puerto Ricans? Will the rights and interests of the Puerto Ricans be protected when they are outnumbered 40 to 2? No!! The answer is that the Puerto Rican leadership should have been consulted by the housing and planning agencies prior to the final formulation and execution of a plan which will affect them adversely.[29]

The Puerto Rican Citizens' Housing Committee eventually became the most important citywide Puerto Rican group dealing with housing. For the first year of its existence, however, it concentrated almost exclusively on the West Side project. It held rallies, fed information regularly to the city's two Spanish-language newspapers (both of which opposed the project), and tried to make its views known to city officials. Although there was internal dissension and although the Committee had no grass-roots organization, it still represented a major step in the organization of the Puerto Rican community.

At the same time that the Puerto Rican Citizens' Housing Committee was formed, Stryckers Bay elected a new president, Father Henry J. Browne of St. Gregory's Catholic Church. Father Browne is a vivid personality—intelligent, humorous, highly articulate, and prone to use sarcasm—a personality reminiscent of the Hollywood stereotype of the waterfront priest. Browne had been a leading figure in Stryckers Bay since its formation. He was now to guide it in formulating a position on the final plan.

Father Browne's position on the final plan had grown increasingly closer to that of the Puerto Ricans. In the begining he thought that the city should build more than the 400 units of low-income housing it originally proposed. He stated privately, however, that the demand for 1,800 units was ridiculously high. By the time the final plan was passed he considered 2,500 units of low-income housing too few.

Father Browne considered himself the spokesman for "the little man," specifically for the old Irish tenement-dwellers who were parishioners of his church, but his greatest support came from the young middle-class Jewish and Protestant professionals in the area. He was able to make them feel that they were not true liberals if they disagreed with him, and he played on their liberal sentiments whenever possible.

Father Browne alternated between seeing Stryckers Bay as an organization for the defense of "the little man" and seeing it as an organization that would represent the majority interest in the area. The fact that Father Browne was now the president of the Council brought these differing views into sharp contrast. Should he speak for the Council as a whole, or, if he did so, would he be contravening the interests of the underprivileged? As Father Browne grew more radical, the Council members grew more conservative, under the fear that any change in the plans would mean more months of delay. Thus, his conflict between the two roles increased. In the end he chose to speak for "the little man."

Starting in early 1960, after the initial excitement over the formation of the Council, attendance at Stryckers Bay meetings began to fall off. It was mostly the people who favored the preliminary plan who stopped attending. Seeing this trend, William Houlton, a homeowner and a representative of the 94th Street Block Association, Sillik Polayes, soon to be Democratic District Leader of the Fourth A.D. North, and several others began in the fall of 1961 to urge those who favored the plan to attend meetings. Their efforts were successful. During the first half of 1961 the average attendance per monthly meeting had been twenty-one people. This increased to thirty-three per meeting for the second half of 1961, and to forty-eight per meeting for the first half of 1962.[30]

CPC released the final plan for WSURA on May 1, 1962. On May 9 the housing committee of Stryckers Bay met under Father Browne's chairmanship. Since the beginning of the year, the committee had been urging the city to include 2,500 units of low-income housing in the project. The city's final plan called for the same low-high-middle distribution of 1,000–4,200–2,800 that the Board of Estimate had approved in 1959. The housing committee, realizing that the full Council would not support a plea for 2,500 low-income units, passed a resolution calling for a 1,900–4,200–1,900 distribution.

On May 14 the full Council met. The resolution of the housing committee was submitted and was passed by a show of hands, 33–26. Someone called for a roll call. On the roll-call vote the resolution was defeated 34–33. Speeches were made about the long delay that would follow if the plan were changed. Houlton submitted a resolution favoring the city's plan with the provisos that a new advisory committee on relocation be formed and that the Board of Estimate specifically state that changes in the relocation procedure would be made in the second and third stages of the project if relocation in the first stage proved unsatisfactory. Houlton's resolution was passed overwhelmingly. A substitute proposal supporting the final plan with no provisos was then put forward. It passed 48–26, and the meeting was over.

The situation in the FDR–Woodrow Wilson Democrats was not dissimilar to that in Stryckers Bay. There, too, the housing committee was strongly weighted in favor of more public housing and against the city plan. The committee was headed by a young lawyer, Myron Cohen. Most of the work was done by a small tightly knit group consisting of Cohen, Nancy Brigham, Alan Oppenheim, and Aramis Gomez. (Gomez had joined the club for the specific purpose of having a voice in the club's stand on urban renewal. He was one of the few Puerto Rican members of the club.) This group, working hard together several nights a week, became jealous of any outside interference in their work. Periodically other club members would try to join the committee, but they were deliberately and successfully discouraged from doing so by Cohen and the other "in" members.

The housing committee started out by favoring 1,400 low-income units for the renewal area. As they continued their work and were subjected to the prodding of Gomez, however, they gradually worked their way up to a position favoring 2,500 low-income units. This was the same figure advocated by the Puerto Ricans and by most of the members of the Stryckers Bay housing committee. In December, 1961, Cohen's committee issued a twenty-page report, which examined every aspect of the preliminary plan in great detail. The report advocated changing the distribution of housing to 2,650 units of low-income, 3,680 units of middle-income, and 1,655 units of high-income. It also urged the city to return to its original plan of performing the relocation work itself.[31]

The stand that the housing committee took was also the stand taken by most of the elected officials of the Reform movement. Congressman William Fitts Ryan had declared that no urban renewal funds should be used for high-income housing and that the amount of low-income housing in WSURA should be greatly increased. Ryan's sentiments were echoed by State Senator Manfred Ohrenstein and City Councilman Theodore Weiss. These leaders, especially Ryan, had considerable influence on the members of the housing committee and on the club as a whole.

Since its inception, the FDR–Woodrow Wilson Democrats had been divided into several warring factions. The club was almost evenly divided on the urban renewal plan. After much debate, however, it voted to accept tentatively the housing committee's report. The real showdown in the club was to come on the eve of the final Board of Estimate meeting.

Approval of the Final Plan. On May 17, 1962, CPC held its public hearing on the final plan. A total of sixty-one speakers appeared. There was no dominant sentiment either in favor or against the plan. While some speakers were totally in favor and some were totally against, a large number stated that they generally favored the plan but wanted various modifications. Aramis

Gomez denounced the project as "a masterpiece of deception" and told CPC, "If you appove this plan, you are declaring war on the Puerto Rican community." [32] He was countered by Jack E. Wood, Jr., housing secretary of the national NAACP. Wood stated that to devise a plan that would provide low-rent housing for every low-income family to be relocated in a project area "would be to give municipal sanction for containment and to encourage the development of a community characterized by racial and economic imbalance." [33]

On May 29 CPC announced its approval of the final plan. It took note of the many changes that had been urged at the public hearing. It stated, however,

Any possible advantages that might result from further modifications at this time would be more than offset by the disadvantages of not moving forward with the plan quickly and expeditiously. The West Side Urban Renewal Plan pioneers a new approach to urban renewal. The great need is to now translate this approach from planning to reality.[34]

At the CPC hearing the FDR–Woodrow Wilson Democrats had not taken an official stand. Catherine Hemenway, Democratic co-Leader of the Fifth A.D. North, had explained that the club would consider its final position prior to the Board of Estimate meeting.[35] On June 21, the night before the Board of Estimate's hearing on the final plan, the club met. Attending the meeting as guests were Milton Mollen, the newly appointed chairman of HRB, and Fried and Ratensky, also of HRB.

The club had just undergone a change of leadership. Wolfson had resigned as District Leader, and Martin Benis, who had been president of the club, became District Leader. Jane Mills was elected president. Benis was against the final renewal plan; Wolfson, Mills, and Mrs. Hemenway favored it.

According to a reliable informant, Mrs. Hemenway and Benis had made a deal in which they would both try to recruit new club members for their respective sides. These new members would be allowed to vote on the plan. Whether or not such a deal was made, on the night of the meeting about forty pro-plan people showed up and applied for membership. If they were given the right to vote, they would provide enough strength in the closely divided club to swing the club in favor of the plan. A tremendous hassle ensued as to whether they should be allowed to vote. The club's Emergency Committee, designed to handle such situations, was called into session. The Committee's vote was a tie. Mrs. Mills, who was presiding, broke the tie by voting to give the franchise to the new members.

Myron Cohen, who was leading the floor fight against the plan, declared that the Committee's decision should be put to a vote of the whole club. Although there was no provision in the club's constitution for taking such a step, a vote was taken, and the Committee's decision was reversed. The new members were disfranchised. By this time it was 1:00 or 2:00 A.M., but there was still a quorum present. A vote was taken, and the club went on record as officially opposing the final plan. Wolfson and Mrs. Hemenway testified independently at the Board of Estimate hearing the next day and explained to the Board the events that had led to the club's stand.

Another meeting of great importance in the West Side controversy also took place prior to the Board of Estimate meeting. This was a luncheon meeting held on June 19 at the Office of the Commonwealth of Puerto Rico. It was attended by representatives of about a dozen of the leading housing and civil rights organizations in the city. It had been called by Joseph Monserrat, the Director of the Commonwealth Office.

Monserrat is a powerful and highly respected figure. The Commonwealth Office probably has more financial resources and a larger staff than all the other Puerto Rican groups in the city combined. Monserrat's leadership of the Office has made him a well-known participant in civic affairs. He had taken an interest in the West Side plan since its inception, but the reports that came to them from the Puerto Rican Citizens Housing Committee spurred him to a new and more passionate interest.

The Puerto Ricans had been particularly annoyed because the national NAACP and the State Commission Against Discrimination had supported the West Side plan. At the luncheon meeting, Monserrat accused the civil rights groups of slighting the Puerto Ricans in favor of the Negroes. He stated that the Puerto Ricans expected to get their fair share of support or there would be dire consequences for the city. The Commonwealth Office's relations with most of the organizations at the meeting have been cool ever since.

The day before the Board of Estimate hearing Mayor Wagner announced that he had ordered a change in the final plan. He said that he had ordered an increase in the number of low-rent units to 2,500, the number demanded by the Reform leaders and the Puerto Ricans. He also ordered an increase in the middle-income units to 4,900 and reduced the number of luxury units from 2,800 to 2,000. At the same time, the Mayor directed the city's Bureau of Relocation to cancel all private relocation contracts for the project if it was not satisfied that families were being properly relocated.[36]

The Board of Estimate met the next day, June 22. The Puerto Rican Citizens' Housing Committee had obtained the agreement of all the Puerto Rican organizations to let Monserrat state their views. As each group was called, it yielded its time to Monserrat.

When Monserrat's turn came, he stated that the switch to 2,500 low-income units had not changed his position and that the project was "ill-conceived and does not come to grips with the real needs of the city."[37] When Wagner questioned Monserrat about his stand, the Puerto Rican leader replied that the total ratio of low-income housing to other housing in the area would be one to seven when the project was completed. He stated that 5,000 low-income units were being destroyed, and thus the addition of only 2,500 units contributed to a worsening of the low-income housing shortage. Wagner pointed out that there was much low-rent housing being built elsewhere in the city.[38]

Backing up Monserrat was Percy E. Sutton, president of the New York City chapter of NAACP. There had long been rivalry between the city chapter of NAACP and its national headquarters. After Wood of the national organization had testified before CPC in favor of the West Side plan, Father Browne met Sutton at a labor conference. Father Browne called Sutton's attention to the West Side situation. Sutton had been totally unaware of the controversy. After speaking to Father Browne, Sutton reached, or was reached by, Monserrat and several other Puerto Rican leaders. A Puerto Rican representative spoke to a meeting of the New York NAACP chapter, and Sutton agreed to lend his support to Monserrat. Wood got in touch with Sutton and tried to get him to change his mind, but Wood's pleas "fell on deaf ears."

At the Board of Estimate meeting, Sutton stated that the New York chapter disagreed with the the national Association and wanted more low-income housing included in the plan, although since Wagner's modifications it was not fully opposed to the plan. Sutton also urged that minority groups be given representation on CPC. When Wagner broke in to say that this was not a matter to be discussed at the public hearing, Sutton replied,

But I am suggesting that the members of the minority groups should participate in these decisions which affect us. . . . I might also say that this issue has presented us with an opportunity to integrate our activities with the Puerto Rican community, and we intend to continue this relationship in the future.[39]

The Reform Democrats were considerably mollified by the Mayor's changes. Senator Ohrenstein spoke in favor of the plan, and Councilman Weiss said he was still not satisfied but was not opposed to the plan.

Father Browne had informed Stryckers Bay that he would be

out of town on the day of the hearing. It was thus arranged to have Madeleine Polayes, the vice-president, speak in his place. Mrs. Polayes read the Council's statement supporting the plan. Father Browne put in a surprise appearance, however, and requested an opportunity to speak. He stated that he was speaking as an individual and not as a representative of the Council. He went on to say that the poor—those earning less than $5,000 a year—were being kicked out of the area and would not be able to afford the middle-income rentals in the project: "We are not dealing with a Puerto Rican problem, as the Planning Commission seems to think, but with a low-income problem. The city is wrongly committed to a middle-income program that is not really middle-income housing." [40] The pull of Father Browne's personal views had been too strong. He could not abide by the Council's decision.

On June 26 the Board of Estimate voted unanimously to approve the final plan. The plan had undergone many changes since its details were first laid out by the Urban Renewal Board. Having started out to contain 400 low-income housing units, 2,400 middle-income units, and 5,000 high-income units, the project in the final plan was to contain 2,500 low-, 4,900 middle-, and 2,000 high-income units. Relocation was to be done by the sponsors, not by the city. After seven years of delay and controversy, however, the project was now on its way to being translated from planning to reality.

RECENT EVENTS

The final plan for WSURA represented a victory for neighborhood-based pressures, specifically the Puerto Ricans and the Reform Democrats. Ironically, it represented a denial of the stand taken by the organization created to represent such pressures, Stryckers Bay. The Urban Renewal Board had set out to execute a project that would be a model of citizen participation. To some extent it had succeeded, but models are neater and simpler on paper than they turn out to be in practice. We have seen the complicated maneuvers and struggles that took place among the neighborhood groups and between the neighborhood groups and various citywide groups. Pressure was applied on the Mayor and the Borough President of Manhattan as well as on HRB and CPC. Each of these governmental actors changed the plan. The complex of group pressures utilizing the multiple access points available within the government had produced a plan for the project very different from what had originally been proposed in 1955.

Following the passage of the final plan, some of the organizations in WSURA experienced changes in leadership, the power of some increased or declined, and various internal problems occurred in all of them. Few organizations of any type are stable over a long period of time, but the shifting population of the West Side, combined with the pressures created by the proposed renewal project, increased the instability of many of its groups.

Many of the organizations in Stryckers Bay had become increasingly antagonistic toward Father Browne as his views had become more radical and he had become more open about expressing them. The Council was already badly split before the passage of the final plan. A fair, held in the spring of 1962 to raise funds for the Council, had been boycotted by some of the member organizations. Father Browne's testimony at the Board of Estimate meeting brought the antagonism to a peak. In the opinion of several competent observers, the Council came close to disintegrating over the issue of Father Browne and the strength of his voice in Stryckers Bay. In the spring of 1963 the Council's nominating committee unanimously voted for a slate of officers that did not include Father Browne. Akers, who had been the first president of the Council and who was the epitome of neutrality, was nominated for the presidency. Father Browne issued a statement saying that he had decided "not to express even an interest" in seeking a third term as president.[41] Akers was elected without opposition.

The FDR–Woodrow Wilson Democrats suffered a serious and perhaps permanent decline following the Board of Estimate meeting. Its membership decreased, and it had trouble finding people who were willing to fill the higher offices in the club. There were at least two major reasons for this, neither directly related to the urban renewal issue. The first was the lack of success of the club's candidates for office. In 1961 it had failed to get Austin Laber nominated to run for City Councilman,[42] and in 1962 David Bromberg, the club's candidate for State Assemblyman, had also failed to win nomination. The second reason for the club's decline was a change in leadership that brought about a greater emphasis on national and international issues and a corresponding decline of interest in local and neighborhood affairs. This change alienated a significant proportion of the club's membership.

The Puerto Rican Citizens' Housing Committee has remained the chief spokesman for the Puerto Ricans on matters relating to housing and planning. It is providing representation for the Puerto Ricans in other renewal areas on the West Side, and its influence has also been felt in other areas of the city, but it has remained a small group of ten or twelve leaders. Few new members have been brought into the committee, and very little has been done to foster grass-roots leadership within the renewal areas. Aramis Gomez is still the driving force behind much of the committee's work.

Both Gomez and Rosa repaid their debt to the Reformers for the changes brought about in the renewal plan by campaigning in the fall of 1962 for Congressman Ryan and the rest of the Reform slate, but the team of Gomez and Rosa has been broken up. In June, 1963, Rosa accepted a job with HRB. Gomez, considering this treason, refused to attend Rosa's swearing-in.

The alliance between the Puerto Rican and the Negro communities, which Sutton proclaimed at the Board of Estimate hearing, was short-lived. On June 29, 1962, fifty Negro and Puerto Rican leaders met and formed a committee to support striking hospital workers, most of whom were members of the two minority groups. A. Philip Randolph, president of the Brotherhood of Sleeping Car Porters, and Joseph Monserrat were named co-chairmen of the committee.[43] After this, however, there was no communication or coordination of any significance between the two groups.

On the night of August 1, 1962, just a few weeks after the passage of the final plan, a riot occurred between Negroes and Puerto Ricans living on 94th Street in the heart of the renewal area. The police had to fire fifty warning shots before order could be restored.[44] It is doubtful whether most of the people involved were even aware of the renewal project, and similar riots had occurred in other parts of the West Side in past summers. It may well be, however, that the general air of uncertainty that pervaded the area as a result of the proposed renewal and the increased self-awareness of the Puerto Ricans that resulted from the long battle over income proportions in the plan contributed to the tension that led to the riot.

The execution of the renewal project has been beset by the same type of delays that plagued it during the planning stage. The many novel aspects of the plan have resulted in long delays in obtaining approval from the state government and the federal housing agencies. Several of the neighborhood groups are sponsoring their own housing projects as part of the renewal plan, and their inexperience in such matters has also been responsible for some delay.

On January 31, 1963, the city officially took title to all the sites slated for demolition or rehabilitation within the twenty-block area. Although construction is still to be in three stages, starting with the area from 93rd to 97th Streets, title to the sites for all three stages was taken to prevent the raising of prices on property and to maintain the standards of the buildings in the blocks within the second and third stages.

As of June, 1965, the only construction completed in the area is a school, Stephen Wise Houses, a low-rent project that had been processed separately from the other projects in the renewal plan, and a small, "vest-pocket" housing project. Several brownstone houses on 94th and 95th Streets near Central Park West have been assigned to sponsors for rehabilitation.[45] Columbus Avenue is still dotted with green sheets marking stores that have been vacated, but several large sites have been cleared and a number of buildings are in various stages of construction. Much of the relocation work, however, remains to be done.

The people in the area who have worked hard for approval of the plan have often been discouraged at the slow pace of progress. There has also been fear that some of the sponsors of the high-income buildings would try to get out of their sponsorship because of the increased amount of low-rent housing in the plan (which, by making the neighborhood less "desirable," will make it more difficult to rent luxury-priced buildings) and because of the increasing saturation of the market for such buildings caused by new luxury construction in other parts of Manhattan.

Whatever the final appearance of WSURA, the consideration of the plans marked a significant step in the city's attempts to deal with local groups. More consultation occurred and more consideration was given to the views of neighborhood groups than ever before. Official recognition was given to the potential power that exists in the neighborhoods of New York.

Having studied three particular urban renewal projects, we must now turn to the task of drawing some general conclusions. What factors shape the attitudes of neighborhoods toward urban renewal? What groups will be active in renewal controversies? What strategies and tactics will neighborhood organizations utilize? These questions we shall now attempt to answer.

CHAPTER VI

Formation of Neighborhood Attitudes

When an urban renewal proposal is first announced, it is often not clear to the neighborhood residents how the project will actually affect them. Their reactions tend to be based on what we shall call "initial determinants"—their general attitude toward the urban renewal program and their opinion of the city renewal agency. These initial determinants of neighborhood attitudes are influenced by many factors—the timing of the announcement, the coverage given renewal by the mass media, the other controversies going on in the neighborhood, and the impact on the area of previous renewal projects.

Once the plans for the proposed project have become more specific and the neighborhood groups have had time to absorb the details of the proposal, the stakes of each group—what each will gain or lose if the project is approved—become the most important determinants of group attitudes. The specific economic, political, and social stakes of the participants will, in the final analysis, determine the nature of the controversy. Before we deal with these stakes, however, we shall examine the initial determinants.

INITIAL DETERMINANTS

The announcement of a proposed renewal project is likely to provoke the hostility of some neighborhood groups regardless of when the announcement is made. If the neighborhood is not informed of the proposed plans until the process of gaining official approval is well advanced, the city government may be charged with trying to "sneak something over" on the residents, and opposition will be aroused because of the suddenness of the announcement. On the other hand, if the residents are informed early in the process, there will be time for groups to calculate their stakes and for opponents of the project to mobilize. There will also eventually be charges of delay and outcries from owners and real estate men whose property has deteriorated since the project announcement.

In Seaside-Hammels, Moses tried to follow his usual strategy of giving the neighborhood as little warning as possible and providing only minimal information to neighborhood groups or individual residents.[1] Even after the project plans had been issued, the Slum Clearance Committee regularly turned down invitations to speak in the site area. The result was not so much hostility as confusion. Most of the neighborhood groups spent much of their time trying to find out what was going to happen.

In the case of West Village Davies planned to obtain city approval for planning funds and then to work with the residents of the site area in the course of the planning process. Thus, the neighborhood would be given a chance to consider the proposal before it had been finally approved but not until after the city and federal governments had made a commitment to the project in the form of a grant for planning. As we have seen, this strategy was frustrated by the sharp and hostile reaction to the proposal. The fact that the HRB had not consulted with residents of the site area earlier in the process was one of the major causes for suspicion on the part of the West Villagers. It confirmed the Villagers' predisposition to regard city officials as a hostile alien force.

In the WSURA, neighborhood groups and individual residents were consulted almost from the time the idea was conceived, and the city went to extraordinary lengths to try to keep the site residents informed. Some members of the HRB and Urban Renewal Board staff felt that this policy of maximum information would prove to be the best strategy for insuring approval of the project. The availability of both time and information was probably, however, a greater asset to opponents of renewal than it was to those who favored the project. The white middle-class residents in the area, who constituted the backbone of support for WSURA, were the people who were, at least in the beginning, most organized and most vocal and who had the highest access to the elected and appointed decision-makers. The more information the city gave out the more consultation there was with site residents, and the more time there was before the project was approved, the more the initial advantages possessed by the plan's supporters were lost. This does not necessarily mean that the city's policy was unwise, even from a strategic point of view. WSURA was expected to raise the status of New York's entire renewal program. Since the project was looked upon as a model, it was necessary to attempt to create a favorable impression throughout the city.

The citywide status of the urban renewal program is important in shaping the initial reaction of many citizens to an urban renewal proposal. To a great extent, the status of the program is determined by the mass media. Many persons, particularly if they lack any direct experience with renewal, will take their cue from the mass media. If the newspaper or television reports have been critical of the renewal program, these citizens will look upon the proposal with suspicion. If the mass media have been favorably disposed towards renewal, the citizen on or near a proposed site will be more inclined to trust the city authorities and to keep his doubts and suspicions to himself.

Even if he is inclined to be antagonistic to the proposal, the citizen may feel that opposition is useless and that taking any steps to oppose the proposal would be acting against the public interest. For many individuals and groups the mass media define

what the public interest is, and if the mass media have reported favorably about renewal, opposition to some particular project
may be curbed by the doubts that the site residents have about
their own attitudes. These doubts may concern not only the correctness of their attitudes but also the potential success or failure
of any action they might take to oppose a renewal project.[2] The
mass media are important actors in the political game.[3] If they
have been hostile toward renewal, then neighborhood opponents of a project may be encouraged to act because of the prospect of support from the mass media.

During the first ten years of the program, urban renewal enjoyed favorable press coverage. After the New York *Times*
exposé in 1959, however, and the resignation of Moses, urban
renewal appears to have lost considerable status with the mass
media. Once the status of the program had declined, a circular
process seemed to set in. As neighborhood groups opposing renewal took heart from the attitude of the mass media, active
opposition to the program increased. The papers reported the
doings of many of these opposition groups, which in turn low-
ered the status of the program still more and encouraged even
more opposition to it. This chain of events may partly explain
why opposition to urban renewal tends to increase steadily once
it has started.[4]

The mass media, particularly the city's newspapers, have an
impact not only on neighborhood attitudes toward renewal but
also on neighborhood attitudes toward the entire political process in the city. Often the media encourage a feeling of alienation
from the city government by giving disproportionate coverage
to corruption or mismanagement in the city administration.
Alienation may be defined as a feeling of being "politically
powerless" because of the belief "that a community is controlled
by a small group of powerful and selfish individuals who use
public office for personal gain." [5] The results of this feeling can
be either apathy or a sharp hostile irrational action against the

government. The existence of such a feeling will obviously in-fluence the attitude taken toward a renewal proposal and the kind of action taken to implement that attitude.

Many of the groups and individuals in the three case studies showed feelings of alienation. The Committee to Save the West Village operated on the explicit premise that the city officials concerned with urban renewal were corrupt and that the pro-posed West Village project was part of a plot to benefit certain real estate interests. The emotional intensity of CSWV's cam-paign and its refusal to bargain with the city government were connected with its sense of alienation. Gomez on the West Side and Scarbrough and Michaelis in the Rockaways also indicated at times that they believed that renewal was being used for the personal gain of public office holders. In Hammels there were two instances of relocation agents being hit over the head with baseball bats by the tenants they sought to interview.[6] This would seem to indicate the degree of hostility existing toward outsiders who were connected in any way with the government.

Certain aspects of urban renewal tend to accentuate feelings of alienation. First, the renewal program calls for the participa-tion of private developers who are expected to make a profit from the project. This mixing of government support and pri-vate profit reinforces the belief of many people that government officials are themselves in office only for profit.[7] The scandals under Moses acted to further reinforce this belief.

Second, the impact of a renewal project on an area is so great and so direct that the stakes of different groups in the area are brought to the consciousness of these groups in a very personal and powerful way. Alienation is in part a feeling that govern-ment officials do not consider anybody's stakes but their own. Thus, when groups find that the renewal proposal runs counter to their interest, it is but a short step to the presumption that the only reason for the proposal is the self-interest of the politicians or the renewal officials.

Finally, "neighborhood" for some people represents the small intimate community that is seen as the very opposite of the big, heartless unmovable city from which they are alienated. When the city steps in to make radical changes in the neighborhood, this move is perceived as a blow to one of the last bastions against mass society. This theme was certainly evident in the West Village.

Neighborhood controversies other than those over renewal will also influence the attitude taken toward the renewal proposal because the various groups will view the proposal in the context of the other issues that either internally divide the community or set the community against the rest of the city. Long-standing divisions among the neighborhood groups will be carried over into the renewal controversy. This tendency is clearly illustrated by the Rockaways. The major issue in the community was the fate of the slum buildings and the low-income Negroes in Hammels. Property-owners' groups and the Chamber of Commerce had been trying to do something about Hammels for several years before the urban renewal project was proposed. For these groups urban renewal was seen primarily as a favorable solution to this problem, and the internal division between the Negroes and most of the rest of the community was projected into the renewal issue. The other divisions among the various groups in the Rockaways were also carried over into the renewal controversy.

In the West Side the more liberal attitude of the community toward the influx of the Negroes and Puerto Ricans prevented the sharp kind of split that existed in the Rockaways. The Puerto Ricans voiced their opinions in Stryckers Bay and also in the housing committee of the FDR–Woodrow Wilson Democrats and thus had contact with and influence upon the non-Puerto Rican elements in the area. The rapid influx of minority ethnic groups into the area, however, was a cause of tension and concern among the middle-class residents, and the major dispute over the number of low-income units in the project split the community between those who were most disturbed and those who were least disturbed about the new residents. The long-standing division between the Negroes and the Puerto Ricans in New York also influenced the West Side controversy, although as we have seen a partial alliance between the two groups on a citywide level was brought about.

The lack of internal division within the West Village and the absence of any radical population change in the area would tend to confirm Kaplan's hypothesis that "organized opposition is more likely to appear in areas with a . . . relatively stable population." [8] In a sense we may say that stable and cohesive neighborhoods when threatened with change will project their antagonism outward against the city rather than consuming their energies in internal struggles. Also, the Greenwich Villagers saw the renewal controversy as part of a long-standing battle with the city. Many individuals in the Village had been protesting for years that the city and private developers were trying to make inroads on the distinctive character of the area. In particular, they resented the construction of high-rise high-rent apartment buildings. The proposed West Village project represented to them simply another encroachment, and thus their opposition was easy to arouse.

One of the "encroachments" the Village had already experienced was another urban renewal project, Washington Square Village, while South Village, still another renewal project, had been defeated by the community. These experiences left many of the Villagers antagonistic toward renewal. In Hammels, many of the Negroes had already been relocated at least once to make way for public housing projects, and they knew that renewal would mean another move. On the West Side, a number of Puerto Ricans (including Gomez) had been relocated from the sites of other projects. The notorious Manhattantown project, located on the northern edge of WSURA, had left a lasting impression on the West Side community. Manhattantown was frequently mentioned by those who opposed the plan for WSURA, and the demand made by many community groups that the city take care of relocation was in part an attempt to avoid the abuses that had resulted from the work of private relocators in Manhattantown. The protestations by Davies and other members of HRB that they were fighting the ghost of Moses had considerable truth to it.

A neighborhood's previous experience with renewal may make clearer to the residents what interests they have at stake in the outcome of the renewal controversy. The more specific their conception of urban renewal, the more specific will be the factors that influence their attitude toward a renewal proposal.

STAKES

After the proposed renewal project has been announced, the different groups within the site area begin to calculate what they will gain or lose if the project is approved. They consider the kinds of stakes—economic, political, and social—they have in the area and what effect urban renewal will have on these stakes. The calculation of gain or loss is the most important determinant of their attitude toward the project.

Wilson has maintained,

The view which a neighborhood is likely to take of urban renewal, then, is in great part a product of its class composition. . . . Upper and upper-middle class people are more likely to think in terms of general plans, the neighborhood or community as a whole, and long-term benefits (even when they might involve immediate costs to themselves); lower and lower-middle class people are more likely to see such matters in terms of specific threats and short-term costs.[9]

In the cases we have studied, this generalization is not of much use. It fails to account for the opposition of the West Villagers

to renewal. In the cases where it does hold true, the differing attitudes of the upper and lower classes can be accounted for in
terms of a realistic calculation of immediate costs and benefits
rather than by ascribing "private-regarding" and "public-
regarding" states of mind to the individuals concerned. While
the psychological characteristics of different classes are probably
important and should be kept in mind, too many factors are at
work to permit any simple explanation in terms of the class composition of the particular neighborhood.

Economic Stakes. The economic stakes of various segments
of the neighborhood are the most visible and perhaps the most
influential in determining the attitude of certain groups. Urban
renewal has a direct economic impact on small businessmen,
homeowners, real estate men, and tenants. Each of these groups
has played a role in the three areas we have studied.

The small businessman stands to lose most by urban renewal.
Small retail businesses in urban neighborhoods tend to be
marginal operations, so that the stopping of business for three to
six months to move to another location may often be costly
enough to put the proprietor out of business completely. Relocation payments to small businesses are woefully inadequate.[10]
If the small businessman is only a tenant and does not own his
own store, the compensation provided is so small that it is more
likely than not that the proprietor will go out of business. Regardless of relocation payments, small neighborhood businessmen are dependent upon the nature of the population of the area
they serve. A radical shift in the composition of the population
will often mean a decline or even an end to business. To take an
obvious example, a grocery store catering to low-income Puerto
Ricans, even if it were untouched, would be most adversely
affected by a renewal project that cleared the area of Puerto
Ricans and built apartments for middle-class non-Puerto Ricans.
No compensation is given to businessmen for the value of the
goodwill they have built up in a neighborhood.

There were many more small retail businesses in WSURA than in either of the other two areas studied. The West Side businessmen were the first group to organize against the proposal and were among the most vehement of all the groups in their objections. There was no organization consisting solely of small businessmen in either the West Village or the Rockaways, probably because there were too few of them to warrant a separate organization. In the West Village, CSWV apparently had the support of the businessmen in the area. Among Mrs. Jacobs' lieutenants were the owner of a local restaurant and the proprietor of a local bar. In Seaside and Hammels there were very few local retail businesses,[11] although Scarbrough included among his several roles that of being a small businessman, and the threat the project posed to his business ventures contributed to his opposition to renewal.

Homeowners in a site area have both an economic and an emotional investment in their houses, and they tend to play an active role in renewal controversies because of their stakes in the neighborhood. A homeowner is obviously concerned about whether or not his home will be razed. If it is to be taken for renewal, he must calculate whether he will receive adequate compensation and how easy it will be for him to find another place where he wants to live. If his house is not to be razed, he must concern himself with how the renewal project will change the neighborhood and what these changes will mean for property values in the area.

In Seaside and in the West Village, the homeowners objected to the proposed project because they did not want their houses to be condemned. CSWV received much of its support from people who, like Mrs. Jacobs, had bought and renovated small buildings for their own use. The West Village was one of the few places left in Manhattan where persons who were not wealthy could do this, and thus the stakes of the West Village homeowners were especially high because they would not be able to find similar accommodations in a comparable location. The white homeowners in Hammels and WSURA generally supported the city's renewal proposals but for opposite reasons. The WSURA plan excluded most of the resident-owner buildings from demolition. The owners saw the project as bringing in more middle-income people and thus creating a better neighborhood for themselves and higher property values on their houses. They wanted to stay in the area and thus tended to be enthusiastic backers of the project. In Hammels the owners were discouraged by the changes that had occurred in the neighborhood, were anxious to move, and saw condemnation as the easiest and perhaps most profitable way to get rid of their homes.

The economic interests of real estate men who own property in the proposed renewal area are also based on a calculation as to what the project would mean for the value of their property. The calculation differs from that of homeowners in three respects. First, it tends to be uninfluenced by any attachment to the particular piece of property. The real estate man will not have to move or change his habits if his property is condemned. Thus, he is more likely than a homeowner to calculate the impact of the project in purely economic terms and to favor the project if the condemnation award will be greater than the sum he could sell the property for on the open market.

Second, the real estate man may be influenced by the economic impact of the project on properties of his that are not on the renewal site. Thus, some of the real estate men on the Rockaways may have figured that improvement in the property values of their other holdings would more than offset any losses they would suffer from the condemnation of their holdings within the site area.

Third, real estate men must take into account the factor of delay between the time the project is announced and the time when condemnation actually takes place. Tenants start to move out, and it becomes impossible to find new tenants. If condemnation is delayed for two or three years, as is often the case, the real estate owner will find himself having to maintain the full costs of the building while receiving no income from rents. This situation partially accounts for the pressure that the Rockaway Chamber of Commerce exerted on the city for the early condemnation of Hammels.

The economic stakes of tenants are generally not strong enough to hold them together as a group. The fact that they pay rent is less important to them than the fact that they are Negroes or Catholics or Reform Democrats. Thus, tenants will be more likely to think and act in one of their other roles than in their role as rent-payers. The one attempt to start a tenants' organization in WSURA was unsuccessful.

It should be noted that community institutions also have economic stakes. Churches, private schools, and settlement houses often have a considerable investment in buildings, land, and equipment. If the institution is not part of some larger organization, it may have great difficulty raising the funds necessary to locate elsewhere. This consideration gives such institutions important stakes in remaining in the neighborhood, although many other factors will also enter into their stand on urban renewal.

Political Stakes. There are three general categories of persons whose attitudes toward a proposed urban renewal project will be influenced largely by the political effects which they think the project will have. ("Political" is here used in the broad sense of that which affects power rather than in the narrow sense of partisan politics.) These three categories are partisan political leaders, leaders of ethnic groups, and institutional leaders such as ministers, school principals, or directors of settlement houses.

For the partisan political leader the major determinant of his attitude is the attitude of his constituency. One must distinguish, however, among the different constituencies that any one political leader may have. The political club that supports him is one of his constituencies. If he is an elected *party* official, such as a

District Leader, all enrolled members of the Party within his district, or at least all those who vote in the primary, will constitute a second constituency. An elected *public* official, such as a State Senator or Assemblyman or a Congressman, has still another constituency consisting of all voting residents within the district.

The relationship between the politician and his constituency is modified by several factors. First, one must consider what proportion of the politician's constituency will be affected by the project and how deeply they will be affected. Second, one must take into account the kind of organization that supports the particular politician. He may have a "machine," an organization that depends upon material rewards to maintain the loyalty of its members, or he may have an organization that depends upon nonmaterial rewards such as agreement with the policies of the leader.[12] How soon the politician or his associates have to run for office is a third factor. Generally speaking, the smaller the proportion of his constituency affected, the closer his organization is to being a machine, and the further away Election Day is, the freer the politician will be to follow his own opinions or his personal interest.

The example of Crisona in the Rockaways indicates that regular Democrats are less bound by the opinions of their followers than are the Reformers, probably because the organizations of the regulars come closer to being machines. In addition to being a regular, however, Crisona was also free to express his own opinions because the Rockaways did not represent a very large proportion of his constituency and because he probably knew he would be nominated for a judgeship and thus would not have to stand for reelection to the borough presidency.

The party leaders of the Reform clubs are particularly bound by the views of the members, for in most cases the loyalty of the members is based on agreement with the leaders' policies rather than on material rewards.[18] The leaders of the Village Independent Democrats opposed the West Village proposal be-

cause the members of the club unanimously opposed the proposal. There is no indication, however, that the leaders did not
themselves share the sentiments of the club members.

Although the division within the FDR–Woodrow Wilson
Democrats over the plans for WSURA was reflected within the
leadership, the established club leaders, such as Mrs. Hemenway
and Wolfson, favored the existing plan and opposed the addition
of more low-cost housing. On the other hand, the elected public
officials of the Reform movement, such as State Senator Ohrenstein and Congressman Ryan, generally opposed the existing
plan as being unfair to the Puerto Ricans and other low-income
groups. This split among the Reformers was due to the differences in the constituencies of the two sets of leaders. The constituency of the club leaders consisted of middle-income people.
The FDR–Woodrow Wilson Democrats had few Puerto Rican
members and did not expect to attract many recruits from
among the Puerto Ricans. Since the Reform clubs drew their
strength from the middle class, it was to the interest of the club
leaders to have more, not less, middle-income housing included
in the plan. In contrast, the districtwide constituency of the Reform public officials contained many low-income voters, including many Puerto Ricans. Because of the split within the
FDR–Woodrow Wilson Democrats, Ryan and Ohrenstein
could count on the support of a large portion of the club regardless of what stand they took on the plan. It was thus to their interest to try to appeal to the low-income residents who voted in
the general elections.

Both politicians and ethnic leaders must concern themselves
with the changes that the renewal project will bring in the composition of the population of the area. Ethnic leaders, however,
are generally not as flexible as politicians. Their organizations are
based on one particular grouping within the neighborhood, and
they are usually able to modify or change their base of support
less easily. Men like Scarbrough in the Rockaways and Dapolito

in the West Village were quite vulnerable to changes in the neighborhood that would scatter their followers to all parts of the city. The clearest example of this is Scarbrough. Had the Negro community of Hammels been scattered by the relocation process, Scarbrough would have lost his power. His church and his political club would have been left without members, his business enterprises would have been without customers, and his real estate holdings would have been without tenants. The intricate network of political, economic, and social arrangements that gave Scarbrough his control over the community would have been shattered. It is clear that most of Scarbrough's stakes in the renewal project depended upon his being able to keep the segregated Negro community intact.[14]

Rosa and Gomez in WSURA were much less tied to the neighborhood population than Scarbrough. They had no real grass-roots following on the West Side, and such a following was not necessary for them to fulfill their ambitions for citywide leadership. Their strength was not based on intimate contacts with the people of the area but on manipulation of citywide organizations such as the mass media and the Puerto Rican Commonwealth Office. Their stakes were based on the Puerto Rican population as a whole rather than on any particular Puerto Rican neighborhood. A move to some other area would probably not have destroyed the power of Gomez and Rosa.

Institutional leaders, such as ministers, school principals, and directors of settlement houses, often have a stake in maintaining the existing population of the community intact. The degree to which this factor influences their attitude toward a proposed renewal project depends, however, upon other variables. One of these variables is whether the institution is autonomous or is part of a citywide organization. If the institution is autonomous—a private school, a storefront church, a settlement house, for example—then the leaders of the institution will have more of a stake in its maintenance because they cannot be assured of another job if the institution goes out of business. They will also be free to formulate and express their opinions without having to consult a larger body.

The degree of centralization of policy-making varies widely, however, among both autonomous organizations and units of citywide institutions. Thus, the director of a settlement house usually will have to clear decisions with a board of directors. The board of directors often consists of people with a citywide orientation, and this tendency will hinder the director of the settlement house from becoming too closely identified with the interests of the neighborhood. Similarly, public school principals may be caught between the neighborhood interests of the P-TA and the citywide interests of the Board of Education. Generally, the more dependent a leader is on a neighborhood institution for his job and the freer he is to express his opinions without clearing with somebody else, the more opposed he will be to any radical changes in the neighborhood.

Those characteristics of the institutional leader which influence the degree of his own identification with the neighborhood must also be taken into account. If the leader is himself a resident of the neighborhood or a member of one of the major groupings in the area, his degree of identification will be greater. If he has worked in the neighborhood a long time, this will tend to have the same effect. If the leader identifies with some particular segment or grouping in the neighborhood, then his attitude will depend greatly on whether that segment favors or opposes the renewal project.

Social Stakes. Neighborhoods within a city differ widely with respect to the social contacts the individuals in the neighborhood maintain with each other and with neighborhood institutions. We may speak of some neighborhoods as having an on-going social system, a system that ties the individuals in the area to each other. To the degree that their friendships and contacts are within the neighborhood, individuals will have an important stake in maintaining the *status quo*. People may lose economically or politically by having their immediate environment altered, and they may also lose socially.

We can locate several factors that determine the degree to which segments of the population are socially dependent on the neighborhood. One such factor is whether individuals have children, particularly young children.[15] The attendance of children at neighborhood schools and churches creates a tie on the part of parents to neighborhood institutions. The common tie to these institutions, plus such factors as the need for baby-sitters and the tendency of young mothers to compare notes with other young mothers, creates a tie to other people of the neighborhood. In such a way a social system with a high degree of interaction, and thus a strong stake in its maintenance, comes about.

Cutting across the factor of children are factors of class and culture. The style of life of upper- or upper-middle-class families tends to negate the neighborhood influence of having children. The upper-class families send their children to nonneighborhood private schools and often to nonneighborhood churches. They are often not dependent upon other local families for baby-sitting. The young upper-class mother, having more time and money and thus more geographic mobility, is not limited to talking to other mothers in the area in which she lives. Such mundane considerations help to explain why upper- and upper-middle-class people partake more of what Banfield and Wilson choose to call the "public-regarding" political ethos as opposed to the "private-regarding" political ethos.[16]

Such considerations also help to explain the hostility of some of the upper-middle-class West Village residents to urban renewal. The Village is unique in that the upper-class families tend to maintain ties within the Village area. They may send their children to private schools, but often the private schools are located in the Village. Because the Village contains a large number of cultural and other institutions, the people who in other

areas would have to go beyond the neighborhood to satisfy their
needs can in the Village meet their wants within the neighborhood. In many cases they have moved to the Village for this
reason.

At the other end of the social and economic scale, the social
ties may be weakened in segments of the population that because
of extreme economic deprivation or because of cultural factors
are not family-oriented. In the Negro community of Hammels,
for example, the internal family ties tended to be quite weak,
and the family did not act as a unit in its relations with the
neighborhood.[17] The children in such areas may not attend
school or church, and even if they do, their attendance is of little
interest or concern to the parents. The *anomie* of the individuals
in the community may be so great that sociability among neighbors is minimal.

It should not be assumed that the existence of a social stake in
a neighborhood always results in opposition to urban renewal.
When the dominant group in the area feels itself threatened by
the invasion of some other group that is different in race or income, the old residents may resent the loss of familiar stores and
their replacement by stores serving the incoming group, or they
may feel that the neighborhood has become unsafe for their children. They may believe that the quality of education in the local
school is deteriorating, or they may simply resent the presence
of "alien" groups such as Negroes or Puerto Ricans. If renewal
seems to offer a remedy for this situation, the social ties will
work in favor of the project. Thus, on the West Side the middle-
income apartment-house dwellers with families were more eager
for renewal than those middle-income people who did not have
families.

The social stake in the neighborhood helps to explain the
number of women who become involved in urban renewal controversies. While the economic and political stakes in an area
tend to be held by men, the social stakes are primarily the prov-

ince of women. It is they who are most affected and will thus
rise to defend their interests. Furthermore, women usually have
more time than men to devote to neighborhood activities. Unlike
most of the men, they spend their entire day within the neighborhood, and this also helps to account for their greater activity
in neighborhood politics.

Ideological Stakes. Individuals may be motivated by the ideas
they hold even when these ideas are not directly related to the
more concrete stakes they have in the political process. Thus, a
consideration of "ideological stakes" is necessary if we are to explain the behavior of some of the actors in our case studies.

The term "ideology" is not used here in the Marxian sense of
a belief or set of beliefs that mask economic or other private interests. In fact, many of the actors who were ideologically motivated appear to have acted against their self-interest. As the
authors of *The American Voter* state, "Strongly ingrained
ideology is one of the few motivating forces that can be seen
to induce a person to act in terms of interest other than his
own." [18]

In the West Side case, ideology seems to have played a significant part in the thinking of those members of the FDR–Woodrow Wilson Democrats who supported Father Browne and the
Puerto Ricans in their demand for more low-income housing.
These club members were mostly young unmarried professionals. Their income was too high for them to benefit directly from
low-income housing. Politically, an increased low-income population would be to the disadvantage of the Reform movement,
although some argued that it was necessary for the Reformers to
try to appeal to the low-income groups and that supporting
more low-cost housing would be a step in this direction. The
liberal ideology of the responsibility of society to provide for
the economically underprivileged seems to have been the major
motivation in their actions. They were encouraged to think
along these lines by Father Browne, who was highly skilled in

manipulating the ideological predispositions of the Reformers.

Father Browne himself may be considered to have been acting from ideological motives, although he probably is more accurately seen as an ethnic leader of the Irish Catholics. His sympathies were with the economically deprived. He believed that they were generally pushed around by the more privileged members of society and that the government usually acted to further the interests of the privileged. There are, however, indications that his sympathies were more with the Irish Catholic poor than with the Negro and Puerto Rican poor. Had there been no Irish living in the area, it is difficult to say whether his actions would have been the same.

In the Rockaways, Mrs. Rausnitz was primarily motivated by the same liberal ideology as the West Side Reformers who backed the Puerto Ricans. While her activities may have given her a personal sense of importance, her stake was clearly ideological.

In the West Village, Mrs. Jacobs had formulated a coherent and powerful theory of urbanism and city planning before the renewal controversy started. This theory is embodied in her book, *The Death and Life of Great American Cities*,[19] the manuscript of which was substantially complete before the announcement of the West Village proposal. Like all such theories of urbanism, Mrs. Jacobs' theory was based on a broader philosophy of the "good life" and of the values which that life should implement. In short, she had an ideology, an ideology readily adaptable to the particular controversy that arose over the proposed renewal project. The militancy of CSWV may have been partly due to the fact that, more than any other group in the three case studies, it had a unifying ideology to justify its position in the controversy.

Other examples of ideological motivation might be taken from the cases. There is a danger of converting ideology into a residual category to explain all actions not easily attributable to the other kinds of stakes we have discussed. Ideas do move people to action, however, and one cannot fully analyze the attitudes of neighborhood groups without taking account of the ideological factors at work.

CHAPTER VII

Neighborhood and Nonneighborhood Actors

We have already covered some of the most important factors that lead groups to take action. Banfield states that "the effort an interested party makes to put its case before the decision-maker will be in proportion to the advantage to be gained from a favorable outcome multiplied by the probability of influencing the decision." [1] What each actor can gain from a favorable outcome depends upon his stakes, which we discussed in the last chapter. The probability of influencing the decision depends upon the governmental actors described in Chapter II and on factors that determine access, a subject we shall discuss in the following chapter.

We can, however, probe more deeply into the question of what kinds of groups become active in renewal controversies and why they become involved. We shall first examine the different kinds of neighborhood groups that have appeared in the case studies and try to account for the degree of their involvement. This leads us to a discussion of neighborhood group leadership as one of the important determinants of group activity and success. Finally, we shall turn to the nonneighborhood groups that are drawn into a controversy through an alliance with some group in the neighborhood.

NEIGHBORHOOD GROUPS

Aside from the benefits to be gained and the probability of successfully exercising influence, the most important factor determining the degree of involvement of a neighborhood group in a renewal controversy is the cohesiveness of the group. The group's cohesiveness on the renewal question will depend upon the relationship between the shared interests that provide the basis for the group and the stakes of the individual group members in the renewal controversy. The more closely related the basis of the group to the stakes of the members, the more uniform will be the attitude of the members toward the proposed project and the more cohesive the group will be. We can locate most of the neighborhood interest groups along a continuum based on their cohesiveness.

If we start at the low-cohesion end of the continuum, we may take religious groups as an example. Neighborhood churches generally do not play an active part in renewal controversies because religious affiliation cuts across economic and political lines, and individuals rarely have religious stakes in renewal proposals. The organizational basis of a church or synagogue is not related to the stakes of the individual members in urban renewal, and the membership of the group will probably not be cohesive in its attitude toward the renewal plan. The one direct stake most churches have in a renewal proposal is the economic stake represented by their building and property in the site area. When this stake is threatened, as in the case of St. John's in Hammels, the church is likely to act as a political interest group.[2]

Political clubs are often no more cohesive than religious groups. Their organizational base does not coincide with the stakes of their members, for hardly ever do renewal controversies become partisan political issues. In our cases the Republican clubs and the non-Reform Democratic clubs played almost no role whatsoever. The Reform Democratic clubs tended to be more active, but we have seen in the case of the FDR–Woodrow Wilson Democrats the lack of cohesion that can exist. The same problem affects citywide civic groups with a wide scope of interest such as the Citizens Union or the Women's City Club.[3]

Business groups and property-owners' groups tend to be more cohesive than either religious or political groups. The economic stakes of the members in the renewal proposal coincide with the shared interests that led them to organize in the first place. Such groups may, however, be divided by a renewal proposal if, for example, the plan calls for demolition of some businesses or homes and not others.

In the West Side only three groups that had existed prior to the renewal controversy played a role in our case study (see Table 2). Most of the major actors in the West Side were groups that came into existence after the WSURA plan had been announced. The length of time that the controversy lasted and the attempts by the city to encourage citizen participation

TABLE 2. Neighborhood Group Actors
(Excluding *ad hoc* Groups and Front Groups)

Name of Group	Case Study	Type of Group
Arverne-Hammels Democratic Club	SH	Ethnic
Borough President's Planning Board No. 2	WV	Community
Chamber of Commerce of the Rockaways	SH	Business
Edgemere Civic Association	SH	Property owners
FDR–Woodrow Wilson Democrats	WS	Political
Greenwich Village Association	WV	Community
Greenwich Village West Council	WV	Property owners
Holy Name Church	WS	Religious
Lower West Side Civic League	WV	Ethnic
Middle Income Cooperators of Greenwich Village (Micove)	WV	Unclassified
Rockaway Beach Businessmen's Association	SH	Business
Rockaway Beach Property Owners' and Civic Association	SH	Property owners
Rockaway Council of Civic Associations	SH	Property owners
Rockaway Health Council	SH	Community
St. Gregory's Church	WS	Religious
St. John Baptist Church	SH	Religious
St. Rose of Lima Church	SH	Religious
St. Veronica's Church	WV	Religious
Seaside Property Owners' Association	SH	Property owners
Somerville-Arverne Civic Association	SH	Property owners
Temple Israel	SH	Religious
Village Independent Democrats	WV	Political
Washington Square Association	WV	Community
Wavecrest Civic Association	SH	Property owners

led to the creation of groups specifically for the expression of neighborhood attitudes toward the renewal proposal. Such groups were also formed in the Rockaways and in the West Village.

An urban renewal controversy may give rise within a neighborhood to common interests that either did not exist previously or that were not felt intensely enough to take organized form. The realization of such common interests gives rise to *ad hoc* groups (see Table 3) whose basic purpose is to influence the

TABLE 3. *Ad hoc* Neighborhood Groups

Name of Group	Case Study	Type of Group
Borough President's "Watchdog Committee"	SH	Property owners
Committee to Save the West Village	WV	Community
87–97th Street Business and Professional Group	WS	Business
Park-Hudson Urban Renewal Committee	WS	Community
Puerto Rican Citizens' Housing Committee	WS	Ethnic
Rockaway Council for Relocation and Slum Prevention	SH	Community
Spanish-American Committee of the West Side Urban Renewal Area	WS	Ethnic
Stryckers Bay Neighborhood Council	WS	Community
West Side Tenants' Committee	WS	Tenants

outcome of the renewal controversy. Since *ad hoc* groups are formed specifically on the basis of the members' stakes in the renewal controversy, the attitudes of the members are highly cohesive on the renewal question, and such groups tend to be very active.

In some cases the neighborhood as a whole may take on a reality it never had before because of the common interest of its inhabitants in the proposed renewal project. This is what happened in the West Village and WSURA, where the realization of a common interest and the drive for a unified stand led to the creation of CSWV and of Stryckers Bay. Neither the West Village nor WSURA had thought of themselves as distinct neighborhoods prior to the controversy, but in both areas there emerged, as a result of the controversy, strong organizations representing the entire neighborhood.

The Rockaways made no attempt to create a group that would represent the entire community. At least three reasons may be given:

1. The divisions between the Hammels Negroes and the rest of the community were so great that no basis for a common interest existed. Sharp splits among the other community groups also existed.

2. The community was dominated by one particularly powerful group, the Chamber of Commerce. Any attempt to set up a communitywide organization either would have met with opposition from the Chamber, in which case it would have failed before it had started, or would have had to face the likelihood of being completely taken over by the Chamber.

3. The Slum Clearance Committee discouraged any neighborhood participation. There seemed to be little chance to bargain, and thus there was not much incentive to establish a bargaining group.

The obstacles to forming effective neighborhoodwide councils will vary from area to area, but there will be many obstructions in any neighborhood, and the creation of such all-encompassing *ad hoc* groups is probably exceptional. *Ad hoc* groups based on more particular interests are far more common. Almost any kind of interest—the economic interests of West Side businessmen, the political and economic interests of the Puerto Ricans, the ideological interests of the Rockaway liberals —can be so affected by a renewal proposal as to give rise to an *ad hoc* group.

In considering why and when *ad hoc* groups are formed, we must take many factors into account. Population size, availability of leadership material, the amount of time groups have to organize, the advantages to be gained from successfully exercising influence, the probability of influencing the decision, and the lack of representation by existing groups are all important.

The case studies also illustrate the important role played by existing groups (including city agencies) in stimulating the formation of *ad hoc* groups.[4] In the three areas studied, at least nine *ad hoc* groups were formed during the renewal controversy. Of the nine, six owed their existence to other groups. In Seaside-Hammels, the Rockaway Council for Relocation and Slum Prevention was brought into existence by the Rockaway Health Council and also received support from a city agency, COIR. The Borough President's "Watchdog Committee" was established by the Queens Borough President. On the West Side, Park-Hudson was set up by the city government, and Stryckers Bay received much help from Coffey of the Community Service Society and later from the city government. Coffey along with Stryckers Bay also helped establish Gomez's Spanish-American Committee of WSURA. The West Side Tenants Committee was assisted by another *ad hoc* group, the 87–97th Street Business and Professional Group. The Puerto Rican Citizens' Housing Committee was established with the help and encouragement of COIR and of the Office of the Commonwealth of Puerto Rico.

Why do so many nonneighborhood groups take an interest in forming *ad hoc* groups within the neighborhood? In part it may be because the parent group fears that it will alienate some of its support if it takes a stand on the issue or plays an active role.[5] This certainly explains the role of COIR. The factor that seems most important, however, is the added weight that city agencies and other citywide groups, including the mass media, give to opinion that comes from the neighborhood directly affected by the urban renewal proposal. City agencies and citywide groups want a group *in the site area* that will represent their views because their views will seem to the other actors to have more legitimacy if they come from this source. Also, the views may be expressed more vigorously by *ad hoc* groups because of their cohesiveness.

A distinction must be made between two kinds of *ad hoc* groups. The first kind, which we may call a "unitary" group, consists of individuals who, while they may be members of other groups, represent only themselves in the newly formed group. The second kind of *ad hoc* group may be called "associational." The membership consists of groups, with individuals theoretically serving only as representatives of these groups and with the voting usually on a group basis. CSWV, the 87–97th Street Business and Professional Group, and the West Side Tenants' Committee are examples of unitary *ad hoc* groups. Stryckers Bay and the Rockaway Council on Relocation and Slum Prevention are examples of associational *ad hoc* groups. When associational groups have achieved enough momentum to be considered as separate entities, the individual members tend to modify their role as group spokesmen. Of the more than forty organizations represented in Stryckers Bay, not more than two or three instructed their delegates how to vote on even the most important questions. One can draw important distinctions, however, between unitary and associational *ad hoc* groups.

Generally speaking, unitary groups are more militant and more extreme in their demands than are associational groups. Unitary *ad hoc* groups have usually not had time to adjust to other groups in the area or to reach any sort of working accommodation with them. Cohesion within the group tends to be greater, at least so far as the attitude toward the renewal project goes; thus, there are fewer limitations on the leadership arising from within the group. The lack of restraints upon such groups may be reinforced by the nature of the leadership. These groups often serve as the vehicle for new leaders within the neighborhood, and new leaders, like new groups, are usually more militant than those who have had experience in negotiation and compromise.

Associational groups may also produce new leaders within a community, but they are, by their nature, subject to more restraints than unitary groups. The membership will be sensitive to demands or actions that might jeopardize the stakes their parent organizations have built up in the community over a period of time. The member organizations may be afraid of losing members who do not agree with the stand the associational group takes on renewal. They may be afraid of losing access to city officials or of endangering their chances of success on other matters not related to renewal. Also, opinion within an associational group will be modified by the probable differences that arise among the members. More viewpoints are almost always represented within an associational group than within a unitary group.[6]

Associational groups may be said to have overlapping membership built into their structure. As we noted above, however, many members of unitary groups are also members of other groups. Even if they are not members of other formal groups, their roles as members of general ethnic or economic groupings may affect their membership in the unitary group. Thus, the West Side Tenants' Committee was unable to make any headway because the role of tenant was not prominent enough in the minds of individuals to overcome the divisive influence of their other roles. The 87–97th Street Business and Professional Group lacked cohesion because the role of the businessmen as individual entrepreneurs eroded the cohesion produced by their common plight as small businessmen in an urban renewal area. On the other hand, the cohesiveness and resulting militancy of CSWV was probably fostered by the lack of other organizations in the West Village. The only neighborhood rival that CSWV faced was a "front group," the West Greenwich Village Site Tenants' Committee.

"Front groups" (see Table 4) are *ad hoc* groups that are established by other groups and that are also controlled, at least to a very high degree, by the leaders of the group responsible for their establishment. The Joint Village Committee to Defeat the West Village Proposal and Get a Proper One did not really have any existence apart from CSWV. The West Greenwich Village Site Tenants' Committee was a creation of Micove. Its organization and most of its membership probably did not exist except in the minds of the Micove leadership. These two organizations are clear-cut examples of front groups. It is often difficult, however, to distinguish between a regular *ad hoc* group and a front group, especially in view of the important role played by outside groups in establishing *ad hoc* groups. Was Kirk acting as an agent of Micove when he set up "The Neighbors'," and can we therefore consider "The Neighbors' " as simply an attempt to revive the Site Tenants' Committee? Or was he acting on his

TABLE 4. Front Groups

Name of Group	Case Study	Parent Organization
Joint Village Committee to Defeat the West Village Proposal and Get a Proper One	WV	Committee to Save the West Village
The Neighbors' Committee	WV	Micove
West Greenwich Village Site Tenants' Committee	WV	Micove

own, and did "The Neighbors' " have an independent existence, though briefly? Such questions are difficult, if not impossible, to answer with any degree of certainty.

Front groups are the result of a tactical move on the part of some other group. They are organized for somewhat the same reasons as other *ad hoc* groups. Micove wanted to have a subsidiary group in West Village itself in order to break up CSWV's monopoly of leadership. CSWV wanted to demonstrate its strength by showing the solid support it had from the rest of Greenwich Village.

All three of the front groups in the West Village basically

consisted only of leaders, and none of the groups exhibited a high degree of activity. Their existence rather than their actions were what made them important for the parent organization.

We have come across several cases of groups consisting of only one or a few members. One can, of course, question whether such organizations should be considered groups at all or whether they are simply individuals acting under the guise of group leaders. It is apparent, for example, that Gomez' Spanish-American Committee of WSURA was a dummy organization whose only purpose was to give Gomez, as an individual, the right to speak in Stryckers Bay. In some cases, however, such as the Puerto Rican Citizens' Housing Committee, the group is more than just a front for an individual—a deliberate decision is made to keep the group an "elite" organization rather than a mass-based organization. In the case of the Puerto Ricans, this was a sensible strategy, for the Citizens' Housing Committee had no rival organizations. Thus, it could claim to speak for the mass of Puerto Ricans without fear of being contradicted, and, at the same time, the leadership avoided the limitations that having a mass base would inevitably entail.

LEADERSHIP

One cannot discuss groups without also discussing their leaders. The nature and outcome of the controversies in the three case studies might have been very different if such individuals as Mrs. Jacobs, Scarbrough, and Browne had not played a role in them. But it must also be kept in mind that one cannot discuss leaders apart from the groups that they lead.[7]

Group leaders have certain incentives for becoming involved in renewal controversies apart from the stakes that the group is designed to further or protect. They may want publicity for themselves or the group. They may feel that involvement in the controversy is necessary to maintain the group, either because the members will lose interest in the organization if it fails to act on public problems, or, more likely, because the renewal project threatens to scatter the group members geographically. For example, church leaders have a stake in maintaining their congregations. This stake may be especially threatened if the church membership is predominantly of one ethnic group, as was the case with St. John's in Hammels and St. Gregory's on the West Side. While it is usually important for the church leaders to keep the congregation intact, this is not an important stake for most of the church members. The degree to which group leaders are free to act on their own stakes depends, however, on the nature of the group.

Most of the groups in our cases could not be called "democratic" in any meaningful sense of the word. Some, such as the churches, were organizations that one would not expect to be run on the basis of majority rule. Others, such as most of the homeowners' groups in the Rockaways, had such a high degree of homogeneity in the interests represented and so few people willing to devote time and energy to the organization that the power to make decisions went by default to one or two individuals who kept the group in existence. The absence of internal democracy resulted in fewer restraints on the actions of the leaders.

The access of group members to information also influences the leader's freedom of action. In low-income groups, such as the Negro community of Hammels or the Puerto Ricans on the West Side, individual leaders were comparatively free to say anything because they tended to be the only source of information about the renewal project. Their followers got little, if any, information from the mass media and tended to be members of very few formal groups. Scarbrough could reverse his position on the relocation of St. John's without much fear of criticism because he monopolized the channels of information to the community. Gomez on the West Side could denounce the WSURA plan even after the city met the Puerto Ricans' demand for 2,500 units of low-income housing. Although low-income groups may allow leaders more freedom of action, such groups are often led by individuals who are not skilled enough to put this freedom to good use.

Neighborhood groups face some special problems in developing leaders, problems that may become acute when an area is faced with a renewal proposal and must deal with goverment officials. Certain abilities or talents are necessary for a group leader who wishes to influence decisions of the city government. A degree of sophistication about the workings of the government and of the influential private groups in the city, especially the mass media, is perhaps most important. Verbal ability, a sense of timing, and contacts with other group leaders are also important in negotiating on the citywide stage. The group leaders we have examined differed greatly with respect to these talents. At one extreme was Mrs. Jacobs, whose political acumen, at least in the West Village controversy, probably exceeded that of the city administration. At the other extreme was Leonard Scarbrough. However adept Scarbrough was in securing his power over the Hammels Negroes, he was quite lacking in the talents necessary to sway city officials.

The examples of Mrs. Jacobs and Scarbrough illustrate the fact that certain areas of the city and certain groupings within those areas are far more likely to produce talented leaders than are other areas or groupings. The leadership qualities mentioned above are qualities that tend to be lacking in low-income areas. Within Hammels there was no one who was able to challenge Scarbrough's leadership, even though his leadership was not of a particularly high quality. On the other hand, Mrs. Jacobs was able to assemble a group of lieutenants each of whom was highly skilled in his own right. That the availability of leaders may not be an unmitigated blessing is illustrated by the FDR–Woodrow Wilson Democrats, which was handicapped by divisions among a large number of intelligent, sophisticated, verbal individuals, all of whom demanded a role in making decisions.

There is a more subtle aspect to the ability of neighborhoods

to supply leadership capable of acting on the citywide stage.
The particular cultural norms that exist within a subcommunity
may actually discourage the kind of leadership needed. Whyte,
in his famous account of an Italian neighborhood in Boston,[8] reported that the racketeers were the highest status people in the
neighborhood. What was a high-status position for the neighborhood was clearly not a high-status position in the city as a
whole. This difference in norms may often put particular groups
or neighborhoods at a disadvantage when they are faced with a
situation involving citywide officials. Scarbrough's religious type
of appeal was designed for a Hammels audience. When aimed at
Moses, they were either humorous or pathetic. What is valued
within a particular grouping may not be valued by the rest of
society. Those who possess the skills needed to deal with the rest
of society may be handicapped in trying to secure power or
leadership within the grouping. Those who have the skills to get
power within the grouping may not be those who can best deal
with the city government.

For most neighborhood groups the possession of a staff, an individual or group of individuals paid part-time or full-time to
work for the group, is probably as important as the quality of its
leadership. In fact, the distinction between staff and leadership is
usually an artificial one because, in the few groups which do
have a staff, the staff performs a number of the leadership functions, including decision-making.

The Chamber of Commerce of the Rockaways was the one
major neighborhood group in our cases that was able to provide
a staff from its own resources. The predominant position of
the Chamber in the Rockaway community, including its superior access to city officials and to the mass media, was due in no
small part to the fact that it had a full-time staff. The other
neighborhood groups that had use of a part-time or full-time
staff obtained the personnel from outside groups. Park-Hudson
and Strykers Bay obtained staff help from the city by an ar-

rangement involving a private foundation and two private city-wide organizations. The Puerto Rican Citizens' Housing Committee was provided with staff by both the Commonwealth of Puerto Rico Office and COIR. COIR also assisted the Rockaway Council for Relocation and Slum Prevention by providing some staff services.

The involvement of city agencies in providing staff illustrates an interesting aspect of neighborhood group leadership in urban renewal areas. If the city renewal agencies choose to negotiate with neighborhood groups, they thereby come to have a stake in the quality of leadership of such groups. City officials tend to equate "responsible" leadership with support for urban renewal and to believe that trained staff workers will help to provide such responsible leadership. Thus, HRB and the Urban Renewal Board in effect provided leadership for several groups, notably Stryckers Bay, in WSURA. The activities of Michael Coffey in the early stages of community organization in the West Side illustrate the very great impact that a single skillful organizer, serving as a city-supported staff member, can have. Coffey's activities, however, raise the same kind of questions discussed before in connection with the city's timing of the announcement of a project. The injection of outside leadership into a neighborhood by the city may have many beneficial results and may be wise in the long run for the purpose of obtaining acceptance and support for urban renewal. In the short run, however, there is no guarantee that the provision of such leadership will not augment and unite the forces that oppose a particular project.

ALLIANCES

The nature of a group's leadership has considerable influence on whether it will be able to recruit allies in the renewal controversy. For example, the fluid nature of Negro and Puerto Rican leadership in the city encourages alliances among ethnic groups. Neither the Negroes nor the Puerto Ricans have a large core of well-established and recognized leaders. Thus, neighborhood leaders such as Gomez and Rosa can aspire, with a good chance of success, to become citywide leaders. To make their appearance on the citywide stage, they must deal with outside groups. The fact that they are starting from a neighborhood base is not a handicap, because, given the housing patterns within the city, most Negro or Puerto Rican leaders derive their strength from particular neighborhoods.

As the past history of ethnic leaders illustrates, so long as the group is still distinct enough to be confined to a few geographical areas in the city, the leadership that arises will start at the neighborhood level. Thus, neighborhood leaders have a strong incentive to ally themselves with citywide groups as a prelude to becoming citywide leaders themselves. On the other hand, the existing city leadership is always subject to challenge and thus cannot afford to ignore a neighborhood controversy that may throw up new leaders. A constant readiness to intervene in neighborhood situations is part of the price they must pay to maintain their leadership.

The high degree of cooperation among ethnic groups also arises partly out of weakness. There is an awareness among most neighborhood-level ethnic groups that they are not powerful enough to accomplish much on their own and that help from outside groups is necessary if they are to achieve their goals. The citywide ethnic groups have neither status nor money. They realize that their power lies basically in numbers, or at least in the appearance of numbers via the maintenance of a solid front, and that these numbers must come from the grass roots. Thus, alliances between neighborhood and citywide ethnic groups are encouraged by the weakness of both.

In two of the three case studies, citywide ethnic groups were drawn into the neighborhood controversy. The Commonwealth of Puerto Rico Office kept close track of WSURA from the time the plan was first proposed, and it ended by playing a leading role in the controversy. Both the national headquarters of NAACP and the New York branch of NAACP also became involved. Aramis Gomez and Efrain Rosa, the two neighborhood leaders of the Puerto Ricans in the West Side, aspired to become citywide leaders. With the formation of the Puerto Rican Citizens' Housing Committee, they succeeded in this ambition, while at the same time bringing outside support to aid the cause of the Puerto Ricans in WSURA. In Seaside-Hammels the local chapter of NAACP played a minor role, and later in the controversy Lovevine Freamon, Jr., the president of the Queens branch and the state chairman of NAACP, also played a part. The intervention of Edward Lewis of the National Urban League to arrange an appointment between Borough President Clancy and Mrs. Rausnitz reveals the interest the Urban League took in the dispute.

COIR (now renamed the Commission on Human Relations) allied itself with the Council on Relocation and Slum Prevention in the Rockaways and with the Puerto Rican Citizens' Housing Committee in WSURA. COIR, although an official part of the city government, must in reality be considered a citywide ethnic group that includes both the Negroes and the Puerto Ricans. COIR is theoretically a commission, but all the commissioners have other full-time jobs and cannot keep track of what the staff is doing. The staff consists largely of Negroes and Puerto Ricans, many of whom are active interest-group leaders. They generally do not hesitate to align themselves and COIR with ethnic groups throughout the city, even when such ethnic groups are opposing city policy. Thus, in its actions COIR is almost indistinguishable from such private organizations as NAACP or the Urban League. It should be noted that the New York Office of the Commonwealth of Puerto Rico is also an official organization. The fact that Negro and Puerto Rican government officials often serve as leaders or important members of private groups is an indicator of the fluid leadership structure of the two groupings.

While the case studies illustrate the frequency with which outside ethnic groups will form alliances with neighborhood groups, they also illustrate some of the factors that may interfere with such alliances. In Seaside-Hammels, as we have indicated, there was a division within the Negro community itself. The Reverend Mr. May and the Council on Relocation and Slum Prevention represented the middle-class Negroes. They were highly mistrustful of Scarbrough, who led the lower-class Negroes, and no communication or cooperation existed between the two segments of the Negro population. The Urban League, NAACP, and COIR all shared the same suspicions of Scarbrough. Thus, the aid of all these outside groups was channeled to the Council on Relocation and Slum Prevention rather than to the leader of those who were directly affected by the renewal project. The quality of the lower-class leadership, centered in the person of Scarbrough, was so poor as to thwart any alliance.

The division between the New York NAACP and the national headquarters of NAACP over WSURA also illustrates the difficulties that may arise in forming group alliances. Although the rivalry between the local chapter and the national headquarters of NAACP was of long standing and stemmed in part from disputes over jurisdiction, other factors contributed to the split between the groups. The national headquarters is not so dependent on nor as sensitive to neighborhood pressures as is the local chapter. Its support, in terms of both money and members, comes from a much broader base than does that of the local chapter. Within New York its perspective tends to be citywide rather than neighborhoodwide, and it must negotiate and deal with citywide leaders. Thus, it is more sympathetic to citywide groups, like CHPC and the Community Service Society, and to HRB and CPC. It may also be that the alliance with the Puerto Rican groups, which opposition to the project offered, was more important and attractive to the local chapter than to the national. The Puerto Ricans are an important force in New York but not nationally. They represent a valuable ally to a group limited to New York, but to a group operating on the national level the support of the Puerto Ricans is of secondary importance.

Nonneighborhood economic groups, religious groups, political clubs, and groups from other neighborhoods are less likely to be drawn into renewal controversies than are ethnic groups. Although the pattern will vary according to the particular nature of the controversy, one can generalize about the likelihood of each of these kinds of groups forming an alliance with some group within the neighborhood.

There is some evidence of cooperation among neighborhood groups in different site areas. We have already mentioned that CSWV gave aid and advice to groups in other parts of the city

TABLE 5. Nonneighborhood Group Actors [a]

Name of Group	Case Study	Type of Group
Artists' Equity Association (New York Chapter)	WV	Professional
Citizens' Committee for Children	WV	Civic
Citizens' Housing and Planning Council	WV, WS	Civic
Citizens Union	WV	Civic
Commission on Intergroup Relations	SH, WS	Ethnic
Community Council of Greater New York	WS	Civic
International Longshoremen's Association	WV	Labor
NAACP (national)	WS	Ethnic
NAACP (New York City chapter)	WS	Ethnic
NAACP (Queens chapter)	SH	Ethnic
New York City Central Labor Council	WV	Labor
New York City Office of the Commonwealth of Puerto Rico	WS	Ethnic
Protestant Council of New York City	SH	Religious
Queens Federation of Churches	SH	Religious
Real Estate Board of New York	WV	Professional
Spanish-American Cultural Association	WS	Ethnic
United Neighborhood Houses	WV, WS	Civic
Urban League	SH	Ethnic
Women's City Club	WV	Civic

[a] Excluding mass media.

who were also fighting urban renewal. Mrs. Jacobs consulted with several of the groups most opposed to WSURA. In turn, some of these groups supported the West Villagers. A joint letter to CHPC protesting the Council's approval of the West Village proposal included among its signers not only Mrs. Jacobs but also Aramis Gomez, chairman of Puerto Rican Committee of WSURA, and Eva Schwinger, the chairman of the West Side Tenants' Committee.[9]

Such alliances among neighborhood groups are the exception rather than the rule. While there is an obvious *quid pro quo* basis for an alliance if two groups happen to be favoring or opposing renewal projects at the same time, it is unusual for two different renewal controversies to be at a crucial stage (such as consideration by the Board of Estimate or by CPC) at the same time. If the controversies are not both at a crucial stage, the advantages of an alliance are less apparent to the groups involved. Mutual assistance may also be a strain on the resources of a neighborhood group, resources that are usually quite limited. The leaders, for example, may simply not be willing to take the time to confer with another group in another neighborhood. Finally, the leaders of a neighborhood group may conceive the controversy as being primarily a neighborhood problem and believe that involvement by other outside groups will simply complicate matters. This, for example, was the attitude of Mrs. Rausnitz when her group was offered assistance by the Metropolitan Council on Housing. This parochialism did not apply to the case of Mrs. Jacobs and Gomez. Mrs. Jacobs was ideologically committed to fighting urban renewal on a citywide basis. Gomez desired to be a leader of Puerto Ricans throughout the city, not just in WSURA.

Outside groups whose base of organization is primarily economic rarely seem to be drawn into renewal controversies by alliances. There is no major citywide organization of property owners or small businessmen. The fate of small businessmen in one area has no economic effect on small businessmen elsewhere. Economic interest tends to divide businessmen rather than unite them. The business culture of competition and laissez-faire may make cooperation difficult even within a neighborhood, as we saw in the case of the 87–97th Street Business and Professional Group. The same holds true, although probably to a lesser extent, for individual property owners. In the Rockaways the property associations cooperated to some extent, although the alliances tended to be highly unstable. No outside group of property owners participated in the controversy.

Religious groups of the same denomination feel a certain degree of shared interest. Probably the major reason churches in New York have been spared from demolition in most renewal projects is because such shared interest gives any single church a basis for a citywide alliance of great strength. Among the Catholic churches, which are probably the most centralized, this kind of alliance has found institutional expression in the form of a committee on housing and urban renewal of the Archdiocese of New York.[10] The more loosely coordinated Protestant sects have used the Protestant Council of the City of New York to bring such an alliance into play. The intervention of the Protestant Council in the St. John's controversy illustrates how shared religious interests can form a basis for bringing citywide groups into renewal controversies.[11]

Political clubs in New York are organized on a neighborhood basis. The clubs are often jealous of their jurisdiction and resent any attempt by other clubs to impinge on their territory. If outside clubs enter into a renewal controversy, it will usually be through an alliance with some group other than the political club in the area. Thus, the Riverside Democrats became involved in WSURA through an alliance with the Puerto Ricans, not with the FDR–Woodrow Wilson Democrats. The intervention of the Riverside Democrats is also explained by the fact that the constituency of one of its leaders, Congressman Ryan, did include WSURA. When the constituency of the club's leader or leaders covers more territory than just that of the club, the club may be drawn into a controversy in support of its leader. We shall deal with other aspects of the involvement of political leaders in the next chapter.

There are several citywide groups whose primary concern is with housing and who will thus enter renewal controversies without forming an alliance with a neighborhood group. The most important of these is the Citizens Housing and Planning Council, which is composed primarily of architects, planners, and the more liberal real estate and construction men. Its strength and importance derive from the influence of its leading members. As pointed out previously, Davies, the chairman of HRB, had been president of CHPC. Felt had also been a prominent member, and Felt's successor as chairman of CPC, William Ballard, was CHPC president in 1962. A second source of strength, which derives from the first, is the influence CHPC can exert over other civic groups. In part this influence is exercised through overlapping membership.[12] When CHPC takes a stand on an issue related to housing, it is in a strong position to bring in other powerful groups on its side. The alliance among the civic groups was illustrated by their joint condemnation of the West Villagers' behavior at the CPC hearing of October 18, 1961, and by their testimony in favor of the final plan for WSURA.

CHPC's board of directors considers every urban renewal project proposed by the city and thus plays a part in every renewal controversy. Although a critic of the Slum Clearance Committee, CHPC has been one of the strongest supporters of HRB and CPC. Its position is obviously influenced by the prominent role that its former members have played in shaping the city's housing and planning policies.

There is a second set of groups primarily concerned with

housing that represent a very different attitude from that of the civic groups. These groups represent the tenant's viewpoint. Such organizations as the Metropolitan Council on Housing and the New York City Council on Housing Relocation Practices generally oppose any renewal plan. They advocate almost exclusive emphasis on low-rent housing and oppose the relocation of site residents. Almost all the tenant organizations suffer from a lack of money and prestige. They are maintained by a few activists and have only a small membership base. None of the tenant organizations exercises much power in urban renewal politics.

The mass media may also be considered as citywide actors who enter renewal controversies on their own initiative. The relations between the mass media and neighborhood groups may take many forms. The prominent article that the New York *Times* ran about Scarbrough and the fate of the Hammels community [13] represented only a momentary convergence of interest between the newspaper and Scarbrough. On the other hand, the Stryckers Bay Neighborhood Council considered Woody Klein, the leading local reporter for the *World-Telgram & Sun*, as its unofficial public relations consultant. They called upon him for advice and could usually depend upon him to get articles favorable to Stryckers Bay into the *World-Telegram* and sometimes into other newspapers as well. If the newspaper (or magazine or radio station or television station) regularly gives favorable coverage to a particular group, one can say that an alliance exists. Most of the coverage given by the citywide media to neighborhood groups is, however, probably not due to such a stable alliance.

A number of factors determine which groups will obtain coverage in the city's newspapers. One factor is the biases or interests of the publisher, the staff, or the individual reporter on the newspaper. A second factor is the prestige or importance of the particular group. The Chamber of Commerce fared much better in the city press than any of the other neighborhood groups in the Rockaways because it had greater prestige and more political power. The fact that Davies, the chairman of HRB, could obtain a meeting with a member of the New York *Times* editorial staff and that the meeting resulted in an editorial favorable to Davies' viewpoint illustrates a significant advantage that high city officials have, an advantage derived from their prestige and importance.

Some neighborhood groups may be able to acquire access to the newspapers by forming an alliance with an outside group, such as COIR, which, as an official city agency with a large full-time staff, had good access to the newspapers. The groups that formed an alliance with COIR, such as the Rockaway Council for Relocation and Slum Prevention or the Puerto Ricans in the WSURA, were often able to get their views into the papers by channeling these views through COIR.

The skill of the particular group is also an important factor in determining the coverage it gets. In part, skill is related to the group's resources, especially whether it has a staff. A staff that can devote its time to writing press releases and can maintain continuous contact with the press is obviously an important asset. Also, skill may be influenced by the contacts or alliances that a group has. The degree of sophistication and imagination that a group utilizes in its dealings with the media is, however, an important factor by itself. For example, CSWV used a number of devices to attract the attention of the press, such as holding its press conferences or issuing its releases on a Sunday, when there was little other news.

The major importance of the newspapers lies in the fact that city officials read them and take what they have to say seriously. Newspaper coverage is thus one way in which neighborhood groups can bring their views to the attention of the decision-makers. Whether the officials will take any action on the basis of news stories depends on the pattern of access prevailing in the city, for this pattern reflects the city's entire political structure.

CHAPTER VIII

Neighborhood Access to the Government

ACCESS TO ADMINISTRATORS

The term "access" is not easy to define verbally and is probably impossible to define operationally. In the simplest terms, it means the ability of a group or individual to transmit its views to some other group or individual. Thus, we may say that in a small town most of the inhabitants have access to the mayor because they can speak to him at almost any time, whereas access to the President of the United States is quite limited because all letters, appointments, and communications are screened through a staff and only a small percentage get through to the President himself.

There is another dimension to the concept of access. We may say that access involves not only the ability to transmit views but also the ability to have those views considered seriously. This criterion adds a subjective element because it is difficult to set up any operational definition of whose views are taken seriously and whose are not. There are, however, certain indications that an individual values the views of some group or other individual. He may solicit the views of the group, he may spend a good deal of time listening to the group's opinions, or there may be frequent interaction between them. These are all indicators of high access, but they are often difficult to discover in political situations.

We are here concerned with the access of neighborhood interest groups to *appointed* officials, primarily at the city level, who are responsible for making decisions about renewal projects. Probably the most important factor in determining which groups will have access is their relation to the administrator's political base. In Chapter II we examined the major official actors in urban renewal and the sources of their political support. It seems clear that those groups or individuals upon whom an administrator relies to give him support will have high access to him, and that the stronger the support given by these groups, the less access other groups will have.

The administrators on the city level responsible for urban renewal, such as the chairman of HRB and the chairman of CPC, have jurisdiction over the entire city. Thus, their continuing basis of support tends to come from citywide groups. Neighborhood groups do not take much interest in problems that do not directly affect their neighborhood and thus cannot be counted on to provide support for citywide officials. Also, the very fact that their membership is limited to a particular neighborhood makes them politically weak as citywide actors. These factors place handicaps on neighborhood groups seeking access to the citywide officials.

The handicaps can be overcome, at least partially, in several ways. The most important way is through alliances, a subject we have already discussed. The groups that can more easily ally themselves with citywide groups—the churches, the political clubs, the ethnic groups—tend generally to have better access to administrators. Those neighborhood groups which cannot turn to strong citywide organizations based on the same interest—the homeowners, the tenants, the small businessmen—have a much more difficult time securing access.

Even neighborhood groups that succeed in making alliances with outside citywide groups usually cannot, however, ally themselves with groups that are part of the administrator's regular base of support. The interests of the renewal administrators —slum clearance, the financial position of the city, good planning, and so forth—are interests that usually do not have any group equivalent on the neighborhood level. The groups mentioned in Chapter II, which provided political support for Moses or Davies or Felt, are groups that hardly ever allied themselves with neighborhood organizations. (A partial exception to this rule is the mass media.)

The advantage to a neighborhood group of an alliance with a citywide group thus does not lie in obtaining direct access to the administrator. It lies in a two-step process that might be called "indirect access." The citywide groups that tend to become allies of neighborhood groups, although they do not have direct access to administrators, often do have direct access to elected officials. In turn, elected officials, particularly the Mayor, often form an important part of the regular political support of administrators. Thus, these citywide groups obtain indirect access to the administrators by transmitting their desires and demands to elected officials, who in turn transmit them to the appointed officials. The success of this strategy clearly depends on how important the citywide group is to the elected official and how important the elected official is to the appointed official. We shall deal with access to elected officials in the next section.

The differences in the importance that elected officials can have to appointed officials are illustrated by the differences in relationship between Mayor Wagner, on the one hand, and Moses, Davies, and Felt on the other. Moses had sufficient independent power so that Wagner was not a vital part of his support. Neighborhood groups could not use Wagner to apply pressure on Moses because Wagner simply did not have enough leverage over Moses. Davies and Felt were much more responsive to the Mayor because neither had strong poltical support apart from Wagner. Felt, however, was less dependent on Wagner than was Davies, as illustrated by Davies' greater vulnerability to the Mayor's demand to abandon the West Village project.

Neighborhood groups are aided in securing access by the stra-

tegic position they hold when it is *their* neighborhood which is
being considered for renewal. The neighborhood groups represent the people whose way of life will be most directly affected
by the proposed project. Under the democratic ethos this gives
them something of a privileged position in discussion of the proposal. Other groups, including the mass media and city officials,
will be more likely to listen to these groups than they would be
under other circumstances.

Also, city officials are forced to deal with the groups and individuals in the neighborhood in the ordinary renewal process.
They must survey the area for planning purposes; and, if the
project is approved, they must condemn property in the area,
supervise relocation, check on code enforcement during the relocation stage, and so on. If neighborhood groups choose to oppose the city every step of the way, they can make the tasks of
city officials close to impossible. Mrs. Jacobs told this author that
she was always confident that CSWV would win its fight, because if all else failed, the members would refuse to leave their
houses voluntarily and public opinion would never allow them
to be dragged out by force.[1]

The strategic advantage of neighborhood groups in a project area, and the policy views of Davies and Felt, led HRB and
the Urban Renewal Board to make themselves highly accessible
to the groups in WSURA. Many meetings were held with the
groups in the area. The leaders of Stryckers Bay were in almost
daily contact with various HRB employees and did not hesitate
to telephone HRB to seek information or to make requests. Most
of these contacts were with the community organization section
of HRB. Under Davies, and later under Mollen, neighborhood
groups in proposed project areas obtained almost guaranteed access to this section of the HRB staff. Thus, the important question has tended to become the degree of access that the community organization staff has to the chairman of HRB, rather than
the degree of access that the neighborhood groups have to HRB

as a whole. An outside pressure has been internalized within the organization, and a section of the bureaucracy has assumed a representative function in relation to the rest of the organization. This is a common phenomenon in governmental bureaucracies.[2]

The specific tactics a group may pursue in an attempt to gain access to urban renewal administrators are many and varied. In addition to working through citywide groups, the mass media, or a part of the official bureaucracy, neighborhood groups may also speak at public hearings held by CPC, send letters, petitions, and telegrams, or try to arrange meetings with city administrators. Most groups will try most of these tactics, although we can probably say that the higher a group's access, the fewer different tactics it will have to use. If a group has established a successful pattern for the transmission of its views to administrators, it will tend to stick to that pattern.

We have been talking primarily about city administrators, but a word must also be said about federal urban renewal administrators. In general, it is unusual for neighborhood groups to be able to obtain access to federal administrators. The interest that HHFA took in St. John Baptist Church and its sending of an investigator to Hammels to check on relocation indicates that HHFA will occasionally act on problems faced by neighborhood groups. On the basis of these two examples, it would seem that neighborhood groups can spur federal administrators to action by using federal politicians (congressmen or senators) to gain indirect access or by working through the mass media or through such citywide groups as COIR. One must also take into account the relationship between the local renewal administrators and HHFA. If HHFA mistrusts or has a poor relationship with the local renewal administrators, it will be more likely to intervene. The power of the local agency may, however, be great enough to prevent or discourage federal intervention. HHFA did little to investigate most of the problems that arose during Moses' administration of the Title I program.

The existence of two administrative levels, the local and the federal, makes access somewhat easier for local groups because it gives them additional points at which the program can be influenced. There are still other points at which effective pressure can be applied. Elected officials, notably the Mayor and the other members of the Board of Estimate, are in a strong position to veto or change an urban renewal project. Thus, politicians present another set of points through which neighborhood groups can try to influence policy and obtain access.

ACCESS TO POLITICIANS

Many of the generalizations we have made about access to administrators apply also to the question of access to politicians. (The term "politicians" in this section means *elected*, as opposed to appointed, officials.) Having allies and being in a strategic position are important factors in gaining access to politicians. The base of support for the particular elected official under consideration is crucial to determining which groups will have access to him.

The traditional base of support for urban politicians is the political party organization. During the past thirty years, however, in most large cities the importance of the party organization has steadily declined.[3] Elected officials must increasingly look to nonparty groupings and organizations for the support necessary to win office and execute programs once in office.[4] As we indicated in Chapter II, Wagner has relied less and less on the Democratic Party machinery and in 1961 broke with the regular party organization completely.

The lessened importance of the Party organization has important strategic implications for neighborhood groups. It means that groups other than the Party have a good chance of gaining access to the politicians who are in a position to influence urban renewal. Such groups can ignore the local political club and still hope to apply pressure successfully on the Mayor, the other members of the Board of Estimate, or other elected officials. The situation also encourages the formation of *ad hoc* groups, for even when such groups are looked upon as rivals by the political club, as on the West Side, the *ad hoc* groups may be quite successful in obtaining access to the politicians. The political clubs have become simply one possible channel for the expression of neighborhood attitudes. They can claim no monopoly on access to the politicians.

The lack of such a monopoly affects the behavior of the clubs themselves. As in the case of Seaside-Hammels, they can afford to ignore neighborhood controversies because of the existence of alternate channels for expressing neighborhood opinion. The split within the FDR–Woodrow Wilson Democrats on the West Side also illustrates the effects of the loss of monopoly of access. Some of the ideological liberals within the club wanted to support more low-income housing in the plan because they saw this as a step toward incorporating the Puerto Ricans within the club. But so long as the club did not have a monopoly of access, and the Puerto Ricans were thus free to bargain on their own with the politicians, the Puerto Rican leaders would not yield to the Party. The most that the club could hope for was a temporary alliance of convenience with the Puerto Rican leadership.

Several factors, aside from the nature of his political support, influence the attitudes of a politician. These factors include the percentage of the politician's constituency affected by renewal, the intensity of feeling about the renewal plan, and how soon the politician will have to run for office. Each of these factors affects the strategies used by neighborhood groups. The group can alter the percentage of a constituency that takes an interest in the renewal controversy by recruiting members for the group or by forming alliances. Existing groups may turn to recruiting members, as did the FDR–Woodrow Wilson Democrats, but the *ad hoc* groups, which start with almost no membership, are more likely to turn to recruitment. Both kinds of groups will attempt to make alliances to increase their support. Perhaps the best example of alliances increasing the proportion of the politician's constituency involved is presented by the Puerto Ricans in WSURA. The groups formed by Rosa and Gomez did not have grass-roots support, and this fact was widely known. Even if they had had such support, the number of Puerto Ricans specifically in the project area was not great enough to be politically significant on a citywide or even on a boroughwide level. But by identifying themselves with all Puerto Ricans in New York and by presenting a solid front with all major Puerto Rican organizations, Gomez and Rosa became part of a significant political force, a force that represented a meaningful portion of the constituencies of the Mayor and several of the borough presidents.

The intensity of feeling of a neighborhood group is conveyed to politicians by various tactics. The general tone of the group's letters or speeches, the number of members who can be gotten out to picket or attend a public hearing, and the frequency with which the group acts are all indicators of the degree of intensity. More bizarre tactics can also be used. For example, some members of CSWV may have figured that the riot at the CPC hearing would impress the public with the degree of concern felt by the West Villagers over the renewal proposal.[5]

How soon the politician has to run for office cannot be influenced by neighborhood groups except in cities that provide for the "recall" of elected officials. The closeness of an election, however, influences the behavior of politicians and thus affects the strategies and tactics used by groups trying to influence the politicians. We may say that the nearer a politician is to having to stand for office, the easier it is for groups that represent, or at least seem to represent, a significant number of people to gain access to him. What constitutes a "significant number" will depend on the politician's calculation of his chances in the election and the relationship of the group to those elements in the community which the politician is expecting to support him. The fact that access is easier to obtain as election time draws closer means that neighborhood groups are in the best position to apply pressure to politicians just before elections. This advantage was fully realized and exploited by the West Villagers, and the timing of the city's actions in the West Village was much to the advantage of CSWV.

In urban renewal controversies, the politicians usually serve as an appeals court for neighborhood groups. The groups bargain as much as they can with the administrators, and when they can get no more concessions from the administrators, they turn to the politicians. Thus, Scarbrough wrote his congressman after giving up on Moses, and Stryckers Bay began negotiating with Borough President Hulan Jack after HRB had refused to yield any further. CSWV sought access to the politicians almost immediately because it realized that its goals were antithetical to those of the administrators and that its best chance for blocking the project lay with the politicians.

USE OF THE COURTS

If a group cannot make sufficient headway with either the administrators or the politicians, it may still have a third alternative—it may seek judicial redress for its grievances. Under certain circumstances, the courts may be used by neighborhood groups to influence the outcome of urban renewal controversies (Table 6).

In some respects access to the courts is easier for a neighborhood group to obtain than access to either politicians or administrators. Once a group succeeds in bringing a case to court, the group's political power will probably be of less importance to the judges than it would be to the politicians or administrators. This does not mean that the power of a group will never influence a judicial decision.[6] The influence of such power will, however, probably be less than it would be in the other spheres. Since neighborhood groups are usually weak when acting on the citywide scene, the courts may offer them greater opportunity to win their points than any other arena of action.

The material in our case studies does not, however, give much support to these generalizations. None of the groups in the three cases succeeded in gaining a favorable decision in the courts. Also, access to the courts is sharply limited by the "rules of the game." The group or individual who desires to bring a case to court must be able to claim that a legal right is being violated or that a legal duty is not being fulfilled. In most situations involving a neighborhood group and urban renewal, it is difficult or impossible for the group to meet either of these criteria. The group is unable to make use of the judicial arena because it is unable to demonstrate any substantive legal basis for getting into court.

TABLE 6. Legal Actions Taken by Neighborhood Groups

Group Initiating Action	Purpose of Action	Outcome
Rockaway Beach Property Owners' and Civic Association, Rockaway Chamber of Commerce, and Edgemere Civic Association	Compel city to take title to Hammels	Case dismissed
Individual owners in Seaside and Rockaway Chamber of Commerce	Allow 1960 rentals in Seaside	Case lost by owners and Chamber
Committee to Save the West Village	Restrain HRB, CPC, and Mayor from designating West Village "blighted"	Case dismissed
Committee to Save the West Village	Have designation of West Village as "blighted" declared illegal	Suit prepared by Committee but not brought to court
West Village Committee (formerly Committee to Save the West Village)	Injunction against proposed changes in West Village traffic pattern	Case lost by Committee

In urban renewal controversies, groups take legal action for various reasons. Usually, they bring cases to court when bargaining with administrators and politicians has failed. The suit of the Rockaway Beach Property Owners and Civic Association to compel the city to take title to the Hammels site, the suit of the Seaside owners to get the city to allow 1960 rentals, and the attempt by CSWV to restrain the Mayor from declaring the West Village blighted all occurred in situations where no victory for the group appeared possible except in the courts. The fact that none of the groups on the West Side took legal action against the city probably illustrates the greater access that these groups had to the administrators and politicians.

While the hope of obtaining a favorable decision in a particular dispute is obviously the major reason for using the judicial arena, other strategic advantages can result from court cases. The bringing of suit can often result in a delay of the city's plans, and such a delay may be beneficial to a group regardless of the outcome of the case.[7] A suit may be initiated to put pressure on administrators or politicians. The court action of the Rockaway Beach Property Owners' and Civic Association applied pressure on Wagner to allow Zukerman Brothers to take title to the property, and CSWV hired a lawyer to prepare a second case proving the blight designation illegal only in order to push Wagner into rapidly reversing the designation. Finally, the publicity resulting from a case may aid the group even if the decision is unfavorable. Justice Greenberg's statement that "as a simple matter of justice, equity and public decency" there was "considerable merit" to CSWV's position was used by the West Villagers to gain sympathy and support even though the court dismissed the case.

While none of the groups studied in the cases succeeded in obtaining a favorable court decision, the court does provide another point at which pressure can be exerted and publicity can be obtained. Neighborhood groups that seek to block city action are given a great advantage by the fact that there are many points in the governmental structure through which city actions can be vetoed.[8] The more hurdles a proposal has to overcome, the greater are the opportunities for a group seeking to block the proposal. A strong and dependable basis of power, such as a party machine [9] or a "public-works machine" like Moses', can usually provide enough force and momentum to prevent a proposal from being vetoed. But in the absence of such backing, as when Davies was chairman of HRB, veto groups can often obtain privileged access to some pressure point and thereby prevent action from being taken.

The ability of neighborhood groups to gain access at different points in the governmental structure and to make alliances with citywide groups and the mass media could be nullified if power in New York were tightly controlled in the hands of a few people, but this is not the case. Power in the city is widely distributed, and this circumstance makes it possible for groups to use many alternative strategies to gain their ends.

THE POLITICAL SETTING

Sayre and Kaufman state that the government of New York City "is most accurately visualized as a series of semi-autonomous little worlds, each of which brings forth official programs and policies through the interaction of its own inhabitants." [10] No individual or group can integrate the many forces represented within the government. Housing policy is formulated and executed by one set of actors, transportation policy by another set, and so forth.

This pluralistic pattern may be characteristic of all or most large American cities.[11] In New York, however, at the time of the West Village controversy and during the height of the WSURA controversy, the lack of integration of the city government was particularly great. The Democratic Party, the one mechanism potentially capable of unifying the government, was badly split and weakened by internal disputes. The Mayor, the one individual who could give unity to the various official agencies, was facing a bitter primary election. The outcome of the election was uncertain, and the Mayor was forced to seek allies wherever he could find them and to make concessions to a wide variety of interest groups that represented potential votes. Such concessions were often made by imposing changes of policy on those city agencies that were politically weak, such as HRB. While the fact that the Mayor could impose such changes indicated that he had greater power than those agencies, the fact that the changes were imposed on the Mayor by outside groups was indicative of the weakness of his own position.

At any given time, each agency in the city differs with respect to its vulnerability to outside pressures. Some agencies have managed to muster enough stable political power so as to be almost invulnerable to forces outside the agency that seek to block or change its actions.[12] Other agencies are subject to many pressures and obstacles that they are unable to control or overcome. The Mayor may be considered one outside pressure on an agency. Neighborhood groups represent another set of outside pressures on the city agencies concerned with housing and urban renewal. The vulnerability of these agencies affects the degree of success of neighborhood groups and to some extent determines whether certain kinds of neighborhood groups will come into existence at all.

The Slum Clearance Committee under Moses was for several years comparatively invulnerable to outside pressure. It was an "integrated system" in the same sense as was the Newark Housing Authority described by Kaplan.[13] Moses was powerful enough to be able to ignore the demands made by the Mayor as well as the pressures brought to bear by neighborhood groups. The only major change in Seaside-Hammels brought about by neighborhood groups was the addition of the Hammels project to the SCC agenda. This change was, if anything, welcomed by Moses and thus was not a test of his vulnerability to pressure.

The ultimate demise of SCC indicates that the system did have weaknesses, but these weaknesses were not primarily in the area of neighborhood pressure.

The Urban Renewal Board and HRB had little independent power. Both were newly created agencies that had not had time to build a stable alliance of power, and the creation of HRB was a result of the collapse of a previous system (SCC), a fact that tended to further weaken HRB.[14] Neither the Urban Renewal Board nor HRB had enough strength to dominate the urban renewal process in the way that Moses did, and they were subject to contant pressure from many quarters. Davies believed that he was bound to obey all orders of the Mayor, and his lack of outside power gave him no choice but to do so. Since the Mayor himself was at the time so vulnerable to outside pressures, neighborhood groups that did not succeed in influencing HRB directly often succeeded in doing so indirectly through the Mayor.

The abolition of SCC thus marked a turning point in New York's renewal program. The vulnerability of HRB and the Mayor gave neighborhood groups new opportunities for power. The use to which these opportunities could be put was highlighted by the West Village controversy. No longer was influence on renewal decisions restricted to the city's official housing and planning experts, the top elected officials, and those few civic or professional groups, such as CHPC or the Real Estate Board, which had an occuptional or organizational interest in the renewal program. Into the opening left by the collapse of the Moses "system" rushed the neighborhood groups, the mass media, and the general public. Renewal controversies became citywide controversies. The goal of HRB's community relations staff, "to keep community relations from becoming public relations," was not achieved in either the West Village or, in many respects, in WSURA.

CHAPTER IX

Neighborhood Groups and the Public Interest

In New York City the role of neighborhood groups in urban renewal decision-making has increased steadily. The development of this trend can be seen from the three case studies. In Seaside and Hammels, Moses ignored the neighborhood groups as much as possible. In the West Village, the neighborhood groups succeeded in blocking the proposed renewal study. In WSURA, the city made a deliberate effort to include neighborhood groups in the renewal process.

The increased importance of neighborhood groups has resulted from the increased political vulnerability of the renewal program. In part this development has been due to local factors, notably the collapse of the Moses "system" and the changes in the city's Democratic Party, but it was also due to factors that worked nationally as well as locally. As Wilson has noted, "The coalition among liberals, planners, mayors, businessmen, and real estate interests which originally made renewal politically so irresistable has begun to fall apart." [1] The program turned out to be less financially rewarding than the businessmen and real estate interests had expected and has in many cases been injurious to these groups. [2] The liberals have become disillusioned by the effects of the program on the low-income site dwellers. As more and more groups have become hostile towards renewal, the program has become less and less attractive to mayors and other political leaders.

The inclusion of neighborhood groups in renewal decision-making is becoming a political necessity. The goals of the renewal program both nationally and in New York are increasingly being questioned, and the program's political strength is increasingly being sapped. Given this trend, the program must find a broader base of support if it is to survive. One element of this support will have to be neighborhood groups and their liberal allies, for New York's experience seems to indicate that these groups may have sufficient power locally to prevent a project from being built. Nationally, the liberal groups are a necessary part of the support needed to continue the flow of appropriations to keep the program in existence.

Even if we grant that it will be necessary to include neighborhood groups in the renewal process, we are still left with the question whether it is desirable to include these groups. Those opposed to neighborhood participation can point to many problems that such participation raises and can make many criticisms of any attempt to encourage participation. Some of these criticisms are valid; some are not. Among the major criticisms of neighborhood group participation are that such participation delays projects, results in the loss of federal money, and contributes to a lowering of the quality of city government by encouraging irresponsible criticism of city officials.

It is difficult to estimate precisely the impact of neighborhood groups on the renewal program in terms of number of units built or federal grant dollars gained or lost. In our three case studies, we can say that CSWV was definitely responsible for the cancellation of one project, while the Chamber of Commerce and other Rockaway groups were probably responsible for the addition of one project (Hammels). There is no way of telling what the nature of the West Village project would have been, and it is possible although highly unlikely that HRB, after having made a study of the area, would have decided on its own not to build a project. Since no plans were drawn up for the West Village, one cannot say how many housing units or how many federal dollars were "lost" to the city. Furthermore, one can logically argue that the money not used in West Village could have been used elsewhere in the city, just as one can say that the money used to build the Hammels project was taken away from some other part of the city.

The same uncertainties apply to the timing of the projects. With the possible exception of the taking of the land for Hammels, the neighborhood groups in our three cases did not expedite the approval or execution of urban renewal plans. It is very difficult however, to estimate how much delay can be attributed to local groups. It can be said that the disruptions in the timetables of the projects caused by local groups were minor compared with the disruptions caused by sponsors and the federal government. Seaside and Hammels were delayed for more than five years, but almost none of the delay was due to neighborhood group opposition.

The resignations of Davies and Felt raise the question whether neighborhood groups can be held responsible for discouraging people from undertaking government service and for shortening the careers of city officials and experts. The answer to this is probably "Yes," although again precise calculations are impossible. Both Davies and Felt had many reasons for resigning, and probably neither would have stayed in office for much longer even if the West Village controversy had not occurred. In so far, however, as local groups indulge in irresponsible attacks on the city government (and CSWV did), they lower the quality of the city government and of the entire political process.

The neighborhood groups are usually "undemocratic" in the sense that very few of them regularly afford their members an opportunity to vote on the stands the group will take. Very often the leader will speak for the group without having consulted the membership. Many of the organizations consist of small cores of local activists who have no significant following and little status in the local community. There is also a scarcity of political skills, a lack of interest and concern for the group among the members, and an absence of significant bases for disagreement within the group. Most of the bases for internal democracy are thus lacking in neighborhood groups.[3]

The lack of disagreement within most neighborhood groups indicates that, although such groups are often undemocratic, they are usually *not* unrepresentative.[4] The stakes of the group leaders in the renewal controversy tend to be the same as the stakes of the people whom they claim to represent. The ethnic, economic, political, and social characteristics of the group leaders are also usually similar to the characteristics of their followers. The leaders do represent their followers even though they may not consult with them. It seems unlikely that if neighborhood groups became more democratic, there would be a major change in their relations with the city government or other outside groups.

The one set of neighborhood representatives who are chosen democratically (namely, the local elected officials such as the City Councilman and the State Assemblyman) did not play a leading role in any of the three cases, with the possible exception of WSURA. The neighborhood groups tended to bypass the local elected officials for several reasons:

1. The local officials, precisely because they were charged with representing the entire area, could not accurately represent the diverse opinions of the particular groups within the area. No single individual could hope to speak for both the Rockaway Council *and* the homeowners' groups in the Rockaways. No official could hope to represent the views of both the middle-income apartment dwellers and the low-income Puerto Ricans in WSURA.

2. The local officials were not in a good position to influence the urban renewal process. Neither Councilmen nor Assemblymen played a direct role in the approval of urban renewal funds,

and their political power was usually not great enough to influence the process indirectly. The noncitywide elected official most often utilized by neighborhood groups was the Borough President, who, by virtue of his seat on the Board of Estimate, did have a direct role in the approval of urban renewal projects.

3. The lack of integration or centralization in the urban renewal process, and in the city government more generally, made it possible for neighborhood groups to have direct access to citywide agencies and officials. Since it was possible for the local groups to deal directly with the actual decision-makers, they had little incentive to deal with them indirectly through the elected neighborhood representatives. While this probably had the long-run paradoxical result of weakening local representation in the city government, it was clearly the most efficient strategy for the neighborhood groups to pursue.

The neighborhood groups that have opposed renewal have been at an advantage because people can be more easily mobilized to oppose a proposal than to support it. The gains that will be brought about if the renewal project is built are often not as vivid as the potential inconveniences or penalties that may occur. The proposal introduces an element of uncertainty ino the future of the neighborhood, and people are more readily organized to fight uncertainty than to embrace it.

Groups opposing renewal also can take advantage of the superior strategic position which the city's political system gives to veto groups. The wide dispersion of power and the number of different points at which access can be obtained make it comparatively easy for a group to block action.[5] However, the overall impact of neighborhood groups on the urban renewal program in New York cannot be characterized as purely negative.

Some observers have commented that the goals pursued by neighborhood groups tend to be primarily *status quo* goals,[6] and that neighborhood groups will almost always oppose a renewal project. Our findings lend some support to this generalization.

CSWV was obviously concerned with preserving the *status quo* as were Scarbrough and many (but not all) of the homeowners' groups in the Rockaways.

Many of the most important groups in our three cases, however, were not committed to the preservation of the existing state of affairs. The Chamber of Commerce of the Rockaways supported urban renewal as part of its program to change the nature of the Rockaway community. The Rockaway Council on Relocation and Slum Prevention, representing a very different part of the community, could not be said to be a defender of the *status quo*. Stryckers Bay, representing most of the groups in WSURA, voted to support the renewal plan not because it believed that renewal was inevitable but because a large part of the population sincerely wanted renewal.

It is the lower-class site residents and their allies who are most opposed to renewal. The opposition of the lower-class residents is rational because the program was not designed for their benefit and works against their interests. It is argued that, although the program lowers the supply of low-income housing, it is beneficial to the poor because the law requires that they be relocated into standard housing. In many cases the law has not been applied, but, even if all the site residents found improved housing through relocation, this would still not balance the inconvenience of being forced to move, the fear of being separated from one's neighbors, and the threat which the renewal plan poses to the economic and political stakes of the lower-class businessmen and politicians.

The interests of the lower-class site residents are, of course, only one of many sets of interests that exist within the city. These residents are not concerned with such matters as improving the municipal tax base or bringing middle-income suburbanites back to the central city. To a greater or lesser extent, the same can be said for all neighborhood groups. Their view of the city's needs and problems is a partial one, limited by the particular stakes of the neighborhood residents and by their general lack of information. Regardless of how one defines the public interest, the conception of the public good held by almost all neighborhood groups is biased and distorted.

The perspective of the experts, however, is also limited. They have their own biases and shortcomings, whether because of occupational training or interests, because of loyalty to an agency or program, or because of political ambition.[7] In New York, administration of the Title I program under Moses has given little ground for confidence in the wisdom of an omnipotent administrator unchecked by competing conceptions of the public interst or by conflicting demands made by diverse groups.

If the views of the experts and officials are partial and limited, how are we to define what is in the public good? Meyerson and Banfield distinguish between two basic conceptions of the public interest. One they term the "unitary," which conceives of "the ends of the whole public" as "a single set of ends which pertain equally to all members of the public." The other they term the "individualistic conception," which is that "The ends of the plurality 'as a whole' are simply the aggregate of ends entertained by individuals, and that decision is in the public interest which is consistent with as large a part of the 'whole' as possible." Each of these conceptions of the public interest implies a different decision-making mechanism:

Thus, a unitary conception implies central decision-makers who are specially well-qualified to know the ends of the body politic or the common ends, who can perform the largely technical function of adapting means most efficiently for the attainment of these ends, and who have power to assert the unitary interest of the "whole" over any competing lesser interests.

On the other hand,

A mechanism which is to assert an individualistic conception of the public interest . . . must select from among or must compromise individual interests in such a way as to create the greatest "total" of end-satisfaction.[8]

The increasing disagreement over the goals of renewal nationally and the shortcomings of Moses' administration of Title I in New York indicate that a unitary conception of renewal goals is both unfeasible and undesirable. A compromise among the different interests concerned with renewal is necessary if the program is to survive politically. Such a compromise can produce fruitful results and has already done so in New York. At least three major changes in the New York renewal program have been brought about by neighborhood pressure: (1) an increased emphasis on rehabilitation instead of the total-clearance "bulldozer" approach; (2) the abandonment of the principle of developing urban renewal sites to their highest economic potential and the consequent use of Title I to build middle-income instead of high-income projects; (3) an increased emphasis on improved relocation procedures and, in WSURA, a pioneering series of programs designed to deal with the economic and social problems of the site residents who must be relocated.[9]

These changes have been designed to appeal to the potential supporters of renewal within the site area and to their allies among the liberal groups and the mass media. The potential neighborhood supporters of renewal are found primarily among middle-class residents and businessmen in areas that have experienced a rapid influx or lower-class minority groups. The mixture of middle- and lower-class elements is typical of renewal sites in New York. Because Title I must allow for a private sponsor to make a profit, the areas designated for renewal tend to be either areas on the fringes of slums or isolated pockets of slum housing located within nonslum areas. Urban renewal is designed for deteriorating or marginal areas, not for hard-core slums.[10] This was the situation in both the Rockaways and the West Side. The West Village had not undergone any marked deterioration or change in the population, a fact that accounts for the opposition of the middle-class Villagers to renewal.

Given the nature of the typical renewal area, the partial use of rehabilitation instead of the bulldozer means that many of the dwellings of the middle-class site residents will not be torn down. The construction of middle-income housing instead of luxury housing means that the new neighborhood created by renewal will be inhabited by people of the same income level as the existing middle-class residents. The improvement in relocation is designed to appeal to the lower-class residents or at least to their liberal allies. Far more will have to be done, however, including closer coordination between the urban renewal and public housing programs, before there is any chance of lessening the hostility of the lower-class groups.

The impact of neighborhood groups on the renewal program also has implications for city planning. The participation of neighborhood groups in renewal, will, in the short run, make any attempt at long-range planning more difficult. Planning in the United States has long suffered, however, from the same defects that urban renewal is now experiencing. The lack of political support for planning agencies has made them insignificant forces on the local scene. To give vitality to planning and reality to the plans that are produced, one must infuse the planning process with the realism brought by political engagement. Planning agencies, like renewal agencies, must learn to operate with a more individualistic conception of the public interest. At the same time, they must be given the political tools with which to defend themselves, and they must learn to use these tools. Planning, like renewal, will not be furthered by insulation from political pressures in the community.

The successful inclusion of neighborhood groups in planning and renewal holds forth the possibility of a new community spirit. Alienation may be reduced because people will begin to feel that they can exercise some control over their environment. The political dialogue may become more meaningful because it will be concerned with issues vital to the daily life of the people. The local planning board may take on the role of the romanticized old-time political club as a mediator between the city government and the citizen.

If this vision is ever realized, it will be in the distant future, and the path to its realization will be difficult. The shortcomings of neighborhood groups and the obstacles to giving them a meaningful role in decision-making have been amply illustrated in this study, but the major problems not only of housing and planning but of civil rights, poverty, and the political life of our urban communities call for new solutions and major changes. We must strive to incorporate groups into the political process, not exclude them. We must give them some responsibility for helping themselves, not make them totally dependent on distant and unseen forces. The result will be a better and more democratic community.

Notes

CHAPTER I. INTRODUCTION

1. See Coleman Woodbury, ed., *Urban Development: Problems and Practices* and *The Future of Cities and Urban Development* (Chicago, University of Chicago Press, 1953); Editors of *Fortune*, *The Exploding Metropolis* (New York, Doubleday, 1958); Webb S. Fiser, *Mastery of the Metropolis* (Englewood Cliffs, N.J., Prentice-Hall, 1962); Martin Millspaugh and Gurney Breckenfeld, *The Human Side of Urban Renewal: A Study of the Attitude Changes Produced by Neighborhood Rehabilitation*, ed. by Miles L. Colean (New York, Washburn, 1960); Martin Anderson, *The Federal Bulldozer: A Critical Analysis of Urban Renewal, 1949–1962* (Cambridge, Mass., MIT Press, 1964).

2. See David B. Truman, *The Governmental Process: Political Interests and Public Opinion* (New York, Knopf, 1951), pp. 33–39.

3. See, for example, *ibid.*; James Coleman, *Community Conflict* (New York, Free Press, 1961); Edward C. Banfield and James Q. Wilson, *City Politics* (Cambridge, Mass., MIT Press, 1963).

4. Wallace S. Sayre and Herbert Kaufman, *Governing New York City: Politics in the Metropolis* (New York, Russell Sage Foundation, 1960; paperback edition, New York, Norton, 1965).

5. Martin Meyerson and Edward C. Banfield, *Politics, Planning, and the Public Interest: The Case of Public Housing in Chicago* (New York, Free Press, 1955).

6. *Ibid.*, pp. 91–120.

7. Robert Dahl, *Who Governs? Democracy and Power in an American City* (New Haven, Yale University Press, 1961).

8. Harold Kaplan, *Urban Renewal Politics: Slum Clearance in Newark* (New York, Columbia University Press, 1963).

9. *Ibid.*, pp. 91–120.   10. *Ibid.*, pp. 138–39.

11. Herbert J. Gans, *The Urban Villagers: Group and Class in the Life of Italian-Americans* (New York, Free Press, 1962).

12. Peter Rossi et al., *The Politics of Urban Renewal: The Chicago Findings* (New York, Free Press, 1961).

13. Gans, *Urban Villagers*, pp. 281–304.

CHAPTER II. URBAN RENEWAL IN NEW YORK CITY

1. The federal government will pay the local government up to three-fourths of net project cost under certain circumstances. See Martin Anderson, *The Federal Bulldozer: A Critical Analysis of Urban Renewal* (Cambridge, Mass., MIT Press, 1964), p. 21.

2. See Robert C. Weaver, *The Urban Complex: Human Values in Urban Life* (New York, Doubleday, 1964), p. 85 and *passim*.

3. See Norton E. Long, "The Local Community as an Ecology of Games," in *The Polity*, ed. by Charles Press (Chicago, Rand McNally, 1962), pp. 139–55.

4. See Wallace S. Sayre and Herbert Kaufman, *Governing New York City: Politics in the Metropolis* (New York, Russell Sage Foundation, 1960; paperback edition, New York, Norton, 1965), pp. 92 ff.

5. David B. Truman in *The Governmental Process: Political Interests and Public Opinion* (New York, Knopf, 1951), p. 37, defines a political interest group as a "shared-attitude group" that "makes its claims [upon other groups] through or upon any of the institutions of government."

6. For a suggestive discussion of Moses, see Rexford Tugwell, "The Moses Effect," in Edward C. Banfield, ed., *Urban Government: A Reader in Politics and Administration* (New York, Free Press, 1961), pp. 462–72. Cleveland Rodgers, *Robert Moses* (New York, Henry Holt, 1952), contains some useful information.

7. "Another public 'type' is the man of action, who speaks bluntly and even acidly, 'gets things done,' has no patience with long-range planners and others who would pause to assess the cost as well as the benefits of proposed innovations and great public works, cows his opposition, and points to his trail of accomplishments as monuments to his ability and proof of his genius. Those who are able to establish such images of themselves and their organizations are ordinarily able to affect the formulation and execution of public policy much more profoundly than any objective evaluation of their other sources of strength would indicate is possible." Herbert

Kaufman, *Politics and Policies in State and Local Governments* (Englewood Cliffs, N.J., Prentice-Hall, 1963), p. 106. This description fits Moses perfectly.

8. Rodgers, *Moses,* p. 180.

9. On "entrepreneurs" of public works, see Harold Kaplan, *Urban Renewal Politics: Slum Clearance in Newark* (New York, Columbia University Press, 1963), pp. 37–38 and *passim.* On Moses as entrepreneur, see Martin Meyerson and Edward C. Banfield, *Politics, Planning, and the Public Interest: The Case of Public Housing in Chicago* (New York, Free Press, 1955), pp. 294–97, and Sayre and Kaufman, *Governing New York City,* pp. 381–82.

10. On the cycle of success, see Kaplan, *Urban Renewal Politics,* p. 35.

11. Daniel P. Moynihan speaking at a proseminar of the Metropolitan Region Program, Columbia University, Nov. 30, 1960.

12. See, for example, New York *Times,* April 12, 1954, p. 1, and April 19, 1954, p. 1. Between 1952 and 1960, HHFA was also reluctant to interfere with Moses because he was building more projects than any other renewal administrator in the country and because the Eisenhower administration tended to oppose federal government interference on the local level.

13. Committee on Slum Clearance, "Title One Progress," New York, Oct. 26, 1959.

14. Information in above two paragraphs from the New York *Times,* July 1, 1959, p. 23.

15. "Building a Better New York," report to the Mayor by J. Anthony Panuch, March 1, 1960.

16. Cadman Plaza and Cobble Hill, respectively. On Jan. 16, 1965, it was announced that Mollen was resigning as Chairman of HRB to assume the post of City Coordinator of Housing and Development. Herbert Evans was named the new chairman.

17. See S. J. Makielski, Jr., *The Politics of Zoning: The New York Experience* (New York, Columbia University Press, 1966), *passim.*

18. Sayre and Kaufman, *Governing New York City,* p. 379.

19. *Ibid.,* p. 378.   20. *Ibid.,* p. 689.   21. *Ibid.,* p. 650.

22. For a full account see Martin Dworkis, *The Community Planning Boards of New York* (New York, New York University Graduate School of Public Administration, 1961).

23. For a set of proposals and a discussion of the new planning

boards, see Citizens Union and Citizens Housing and Planning Council, "A Program for Community Districts" (New York, June, 1964).

24. *U.S. Government Organization Manual, 1961–62* (Washington, D.C., 1961), p. 438.

25. HHFA, "Program for Community Improvement" (Washington, D.C., August, 1960), p. 4.

26. Webb S. Fiser, *Mastery of the Metropolis* (Englewood Cliffs, N.J., Prentice-Hall, 1962), p. 90.

27. See, for example, New York *Times*, April 19, 1954, p. 1.

28. On integration in urban renewal systems, see Kaplan, *Urban Renewal Politics*, pp. 165–83. On New York City's political structure, see Sayre and Kaufman, *Governing New York City, passim.*

CHAPTER III. SEASIDE-HAMMELS

1. New York City Planning Commission, Dept. of City Planning, "Initial Report on Planning Area 423" (June, 1962), p. 2 (CPC Files).

2. *Ibid.*, p. 3.   3. *Ibid.*, p. 8.   4. *Ibid.*, p. 5.

5. *Ibid.*, p. 24.   6. *Ibid.*, p. 20.

7. HRB Files, May 22 and 23, 1953.

8. Robert Moses, "Housing and Recreation," New York, 1938.

9. HRB Files, Sept. 21, 1953.   10. *Ibid.*, Dec. 4, 1953.

11. *The Wave*, Dec. 17, 1953.

12. Kolde to Moses, HRB Files, Feb. 15, 1954.

13. HRB Files, Feb. 10, 1954.   14. *Ibid.*, Feb. 18, 1954.

15. See memo, Moses to Spargo, HRB Files, May 18, 1954.

16. HRB Files, Feb. 25, 1954.   17. *Ibid.*, March 3, 1954.

18. *Ibid.*, March 17, 1954.   19. *Ibid.*, March 23, 1954.

20. *The Wave*, April 22, 1954.

21. HRB Files, May 14, 1954.

22. Memo, Lebwohl to Spargo, HRB Files, May 18, 1954.

23. *The Wave*, April 8, 1954.   24. *Ibid.*

25. HRB Files, March 17, 1954.

26. New York *Times*, June 17, 1954.

27. *The Wave*, June 3, 1954.   28. *Ibid.*, June 17, 1954.

29. HRB Files, Jan. 13, 1955.

30. New York *Times*, Feb. 27, 1958, p. 29.

31. Memo, Lebwohl to Spargo, HRB Files, Feb. 5, 1957.
32. New York *Times*, Feb. 12, 1957, p. 29.
33. *Ibid.*, Aug. 6, 1957, p. 29.
34. *Ibid.*, Dec. 8, 1957, Sec. I, p. 135.   35. *Ibid.*
36. New York *Times*, Feb. 27, 1958, Sec. I, p. 29.
37. *Ibid.*, Nov. 22, 1958, p. 24.
38. HRB Files, March 2, 1959.
39. New York *Times*, April 11, 1959, Sec. I, p. 23.
40. *Ibid.*, May 14, 1959, p. 36.
41. Moses to Viola Haskell, HRB Files, Nov. 20, 1959.
42. Solomon to Davies, HRB Files, Feb. 28, 1960.
43. New York City Dept. of Buildings Files.
44. Letter to Felt, CPC Files, Oct. 9, 1958.
45. No copy of Moses' reply could be found in HRB Files.
    46. HRB Files, Feb. 19, 1957.   47. *Ibid.*, Feb. 21, 1957.
48. *Ibid.*, Feb. 20, 1957.
49. See Ehlers to Scarbrough, HRB Files, June 7, 1957.
50. HRB Files, July 30, 1957.   51. *Ibid.*, June 21, 1957.
52. *Ibid.*, June 25, 1957.
53. Memo, Botwin to Lebwohl, HRB Files, May 16, 1958.
54. CPC Files, Oct. 17, 1958.
55. Elliott to Felt, CPC Files, Oct. 10, 1960.
56. Hirsch to Felt, CPC Files, Nov. 7, 1960.   57. *Ibid.*
58. See Tschantz to Felt, CPC Files, Nov. 12, 1960, and Beer to Felt, *ibid.*, Nov. 13, 1960.
59. Michaelis to Felt, CPC Files, Nov. 13, 1960.
60. SCC, "Hammels Rockaway Title One Project," November, 1959.
61. New York *Post*, June 28, 1961.
62. Information given to the author by Maurice Callender, Assistant to the Commissioner of Relocation.
63. *The Wave*, April 15, 1954.
64. Russo to Moses, HRB Files, Nov. 17, 1956.
65. Dumpson to Wolpert, HRB Files, Nov. 17, 1956.
66. Michaelis to Moses, HRB Files, Sept. 17, 1958.
67. New York *Times*, Oct. 4, 1958, p. 42.
68. *Ibid.*, Nov. 11, 1959, p. 37.
69. Memo, Nieves to Horne, COIR Files, June 28, 1961.
70. New York *Times*, March 8, 1960, p. 35.
71. Memo, Seaver to Davies, HRB Files, Nov. 21, 1960.

72. New York *Journal-American,* Nov. 18, 1960.

73. See memo, Seaver to Davies, HRB Files, Nov. 18, 1960.

74. Obtained from Maurice Callender.

75. *The Wave,* March 15, 1962.

76. Interview with Jules Michaelis, Jan. 9, 1963.

77. Speech, April 23, 1962, COIR Files.

78. Freamon to Madison Jones, COIR Files, June 14, 1962.

79. Obtained from Maurice Callender.

80. See, for example, New York *Times,* Aug. 24, 1962, p. 1.

CHAPTER IV. WEST VILLAGE

1. Federal Writers' Project of the Works Progress Administration, *New York Panorama,* American Guide Series (New York, Random House, 1938), p. 104.

2. Caroline Ware, *Greenwich Village 1920–1930: A Comment on American Civilization in the Post-War Years* (Boston, Houghton Mifflin, 1935), pp. 203 ff.

3. See Malcolm Cowley, *Exile's Return: A Narrative of Ideas* (New York, Norton, 1934), *passim.*

4. Marc Schleifer, "The Village," *Dissent,* Summer, 1961, pp. 360–65.

5. See James Q. Wilson, *The Amateur Democrat: Club Politics in Three Cities* (Chicago, University of Chicago Press, 1962), pp. 258–68.

6. "You and VID," New York, n.d.

7. "Report of the City Planning Commission on the Designation of the West Village Area," New York, October, 1961, p. 10.

8. CSWV, "Survey of Housing and Business Characteristics of the West Greenwich Village Area," New York, April, 1961.

9. "Report of the City Planning Commission," p. 10.

10. CSWV, "Survey of Housing."   11. *Ibid.*

12. New York *Times,* Oct. 2, 1958, p. 27.

13. *Ibid.,* May 17, 1959, p. 78.   14. HRB Files, April 19, 1960.

15. *Ibid.,* July 15, 1960.   16. *Ibid.,* July 28, 1960.

17. See *Micove Newsletter,* I (June, 1960).

18. New York *Times,* Sept. 16, 1960, p. 63.

19. See "On Proposed Urban Renewal Areas—Greenwich Village," memo from Dept. of City Planning to HRB, January, 1961, HRB Files.

20. See memo, HRB Files, Nov. 7, 1960 (mimeographed).

21. *Ibid.*

22. See memo, Harry Taylor to Moses, HRB Files, May 23, 1950.

23. Memo, Moses to George Spargo, HRB Files, May 24, 1950.

24. See "On Proposed Urban Renewal Areas," pp. 1, 6.

25. HRB Files.   26. Press release, HRB Files, Feb. 20, 1961.

27. Published as *The Death and Life of Great American Cities* (New York, Random House, 1961; paperback edition, New York, Vintage Books, 1963).

28. New York *Times*, Feb. 27, 1961, p. 29.

29. *Ibid.*, Feb. 24, 1961, p. 31.

30. Dodelson did not sympathize with the tactics of Mrs. Jacobs and her cohorts. He soon dropped out of the picture. In 1962 the Greenwich Village West Council was formally merged with the West Village Committee.

31. New York *Times*, Feb. 27, 1961, p. 29.

32. Letter to William Ogden of the New York *Times*, HRB Files, March 2, 1961.

33. Szold to Davies, HRB Files, March 2, 1961.

34. New York *Times*, March 8, 1961, p. 28.

35. See *ibid.*, March 14, 1961, p. 26.

36. Szold to Davies, HRB Files, March 2, 1961.

37. New York *Times*, March 14, 1961, p. 26.

38. Memo, Kempton to Seaver and Ratensky, HRB Files, March 27, 1961.

39. *Village Voice*, March 9, 1961, p. 1.

40. Memo, Kempton to Seaver and Ratensky, HRB Files, March 27, 1961.

41. *Ibid.*   42. New York *Times*, March 13, 1961, p. 31.

43. *Real Estate Board of New York Reporter*, March 20, 1961.

44. *VID News*, March 1961.   45. HRB Files, March 14, 1961.

46. Letter to Fried, HRB Files, March 8, 1961.

47. New York *Times*, Feb. 1, 1961, p. 1.

48. *Ibid.*, March 19, 1961, p. 39.

49. *Ibid.*, March 22, 1961, p. 23.

50. HRB Files, April 12, 1961.

51. New York *Times*, May 3, 1961, p. 36.

52. HRB Files, April 25, 1961.

53. New York *Times*, May 3, 1961, p. 30.

54. Copies of the replies are in HRB Files.

55. *Villager* and *Village Voice*, April 13, 1961.

56. W. D. Littell, "Embattled Villagers Defend 'Home,'" New York *Herald Tribune*, April 28, 1961.

57. Sections 402–03.   58. New York *Post*, May 16, 1961.

59. CPC, "New York City—Urban Renewal Progress," May, 1961.

60. New York *Times*, May 8, 1961, p. 40.

61. *Ibid.*, May 9, 1961, p. 36.   62. *Ibid.*, May 10, 1961, p. 34.

63. *Village Voice*, May 18, 1961, p. 1.

64. A tape recording of the entire hearing is on file at the City Planning Commission. It is the source for the following paragraphs.

65. New York *Times*, June 19, 1961, p. 29.

66. *Saturday Evening Post*, July 20, 1961.

67. "Speaking Out," *Saturday Evening Post*, Oct. 14, 1961, pp. 12 f.

68. Starr to Lash, CHPC Files, July 26, 1961.

69. New York *Times*, Oct. 21, 1961, p. 68.

70. *Ibid.*, Aug. 20, 1961, Sec. I, p. 64.   71. *Ibid.*

72. New York *Times*, Aug. 18, 1961, p. 23.

73. *Ibid.*, Aug. 29, 1961, p. 22.

74. *Ibid.*, Sept. 7, 1961, p. 31.   75. *Ibid.*, Oct. 19, 1961, p. 1.

76. *Ibid.*   77. New York *Times*, Oct. 20, 1961, p. 68.

78. *Ibid.*, Oct. 19, 1963, p. 1.   79. *Ibid.*, Oct. 25, 1961, p. 39.

80. "Report of the City Planning Commission on the Designation of the West Village Area," p. 5.

81. New York *Times*, Nov. 26, 1961, Sec. I, p. 87.

82. *Ibid.*, Nov. 29, 1961, p. 43.

83. *Ibid.*, Dec. 12, 1961, Sec. I, p. 69.   84. CPC Files.

85. Account of the meeting is taken from *West Village Committee Newletter*, II (March 10, 1962).

86. *Ibid.*   87. See New York *Times*, May 6, 1963, p. 1.

88. *Village Voice*, May 5, 1965.

89. *West Village Committee Newsletter*, II (April 6, 1962).

CHAPTER V. THE WEST SIDE URBAN RENEWAL AREA

1. This and the following historical description are taken primarily from CPC, "Urban Renewal" (New York, April, 1958), pp. 14–17.

2. *Ibid.*, p. 24.   3. *Ibid.*, p. 23.

4. Later renamed West Park and, finally, Park West Village.

5. SCC, "Title One Progress," New York, Oct. 26, 1959, p. 25.

6. These generalizations are based on research conducted by the author. See also James Q. Wilson, *The Amateur Democrat: Club Politics in Three Cities* (Chicago, University of Chicago Press, 1962), and Peter Kobrak, "The New Urban Reformer," M.A. thesis, Dept. of Government, Yale University, 1962.

7. Wilson, *Amateur Democrat,* pp. 196, 210, 238.

8. *Ibid.,* p. 238.   9. New York *Times,* Dec. 27, 1955, p. 1.

10. See *ibid.,* Dec. 16, 1956, Sec. VIII, p. 1.

11. CPC, "Urban Renewal."   12. *Ibid.,* p. 40.

13. CCGNY, "Citizen Participation in the WSURA," report to HRB, July, 1961, HRB Files (mimeographed), p. 7.

14. CPC, "Urban Renewal," pp. 88–89.

15. Office of the Mayor, press release, Jan. 27, 1959, HRB Files.

16. New York *Times,* June 16, 1959, p. 1.   17. *Ibid.*

18. CCGNY, "Citizen Participation," p. 1.   19. *Ibid.,* p. 8.

20. "A Proposal for a Project to Develop Citizen Participation in the WSURA" (from CCGNY to Lavanburg Foundation), Nov. 1, 1958, pp. 4–5. Copy in files of Stryckers Bay Neighborhood Council.

21. See minutes of the meeting of the Provisional Council, Oct. 12, 1959. Copy in files of Stryckers Bay Neighborhood Council.

22. Shirley Varmette, "The Role of Stryckers Bay Neighborhood Council in Urban Renewal," M.A. thesis, Dept. of Sociology, Hunter College, 1961, p. 44.

23. Another advisory committee on relocation was later established.

24. Kobrak, "New Urban Reformer," p. 122.

25. See Ascher to Wagner, HRB Files, Nov. 24, 1961.

26. "Relocation in New York City," report to the Mayor by J. Anthony Panuch, Dec. 15, 1959.

27. "Building a Better New York," report to the Mayor by J. Anthony Panuch, March 1, 1960.

28. "Report of the Puerto Rican Citizens Housing Committee," January, 1962 (mimeo), p. 5. Copy in author's possession.

29. *Ibid.,* p. 9.

30. Figures computed by author from minutes of the meetings. The number of organizations in the council did not change during this period.

31. FDR–Woodrow Wilson Housing Committee, "Report on the City's Final Plan on West Side Urban Renewal" (mimeographed, n.d.; copy in author's possession).

32. Author's notes taken at hearing.

33. New York *Times*, May 18, 1962, p. 21.

34. "Report of the City Planning Commission on the WSURA Final Plan," May 9, 1962, p. 12.

35. Author's notes taken at hearing.

36. New York *Times*, June 22, 1962, p. 11.

37. *Ibid.*, June 23, 1962, p. 24.

38. This and the following account of the Board of Estimate meeting are taken from detailed notes made by Debbie Rosenfield of Hunter College.

39. *Ibid.*   40. *Ibid.*

41. Letter from Father Browne to Stryckers Bay Neighborhood Council, May 16, 1963 (mimeographed; copy in files of the Council).

42. New York *Times*, April 14, 1961, p. 31, and May 21, 1961, Sec. I, p. 63.

43. *Ibid.*, June 30, 1962, p. 21.   44. *Ibid.*, Oct. 2, 1962, p. 15.

45. *Ibid.*, June 27, 1965, Sec. I, p. 51.

CHAPTER VI. FORMATION OF NEIGHBORHOOD ATTITUDES

1. This is similar to the strategy employed by the Newark Housing Authority. See Harold Kaplan, *Urban Renewal Politics: Slum Clearance in Newark* (New York, Columbia University Press, 1963), pp. 28–30.

2. See *ibid.*, p. 137.

3. See Wallace S. Sayre and Herbert Kaufman, *Governing New York City: Politics in the Metropolis* (New York, Russell Sage Foundation, 1960; paperback edition, New York, Norton, 1965), pp. 81–86, 491–93.

4. See Kaplan, *Urban Renewal Politics*, p. 35.

5. Murray Levin, *The Alienated Voter: Politics in Boston* (New York, Holt, 1960), p. 58.

6. Hammels file, COIR Files.

7. Herbert J. Gans, *The Urban Villagers: Group and Class in the Life of Italian-Americans* (New York, Free Press, 1962), p. 291.

8. Kaplan, *Urban Renewal Politics*, p. 136.

9. James Q. Wilson, "Planning and Politics: Citizen Participation in Urban Renewal," *Journal of the American Institute of Planners*, XXIX (November, 1963), 245.

10. The amount of payments has been somewhat increased in the last couple of years but is still inadequate.

11. There were an undetermined number of bars in Seaside. The owners formed no organization, perhaps because they despaired of winning any public support.

12. See Edward Banfield and James Q. Wilson, *City Politics* (Cambridge, Mass., MIT Press, 1963), pp. 115–27 and *passim.*, for an elaboration of this distinction.

13. James Q. Wilson, *The Amateur Democrat: Club Politics in Three Cities* (Chicago, University of Chicago Press, 1962), pp. 164–88.

14. The interest of ethnic leaders in maintaining segregation is pointed out in Banfield and Wilson, *City Politics*, pp. 299–300.

15. See Frank L. Sweetser, Jr., "Neighborhood Acquaintance and Association," Ph.D. thesis, Columbia University, 1941, pp. 75–76, and Robert Park, *Human Communities: The City and Human Ecology* (New York, Free Press, 1952), pp. 64–65.

16. Banfield and Wilson, *City Politics*, Chap. 16.

17. On family life in Hammels, see Grace Hewell, "Neighborhood Health Improvement through Functional Community Organization," D.Ed. thesis, Teachers College, Columbia University, 1958, Appendix B. On Negro family life generally see Nathan Glazer and Daniel P. Moynihan, *Beyond the Melting Pot: The Negroes, Puerto Ricans, Jews, Italians, and Irish of New York City* (Cambridge, Mass., MIT Press, 1963), pp. 50–53.

18. Angus Campbell et al., *The American Voter* (New York, Wiley, 1960), p. 206.

19. New York, Random House, 1961; paperback edition, Vintage Books, 1963.

CHAPTER VII. NEIGHBORHOOD AND
NONNEIGHBORHOOD ACTORS

1. Edward C. Banfield, *Political Influence* (New York, Free Press, 1961), p. 333.

2. David B. Truman, *The Governmental Process: Political Interests and Public Opinion* (New York, Knopf, 1951), p. 37.

3. See Banfield, *Political Influence*, p. 269.   4. See *ibid.*

5. *Ibid.*   6. See Truman, *Governmental Process*, pp. 159–67.

7. *Ibid.*, pp. 188–93.

8. William F. Whyte, *Street Corner Society: The Social Structure of an Italian Slum* (Chicago, University of Chicago Press, 1955), 2d ed.

9. New York *Times*, March 28, 1961, p. 40.

10. *Ibid.*, May 5, 1961, p. 18.

11. See Henry Pratt, "The Protestant Council of the City of New York as a Political Interest Group," unpublished Ph.D. thesis, Department of Public Law and Government, Columbia University, 1963.

12. Of the sixty persons who were on the CHPC Board of Directors in 1962, seven were also on the board of United Neighborhood Houses, the group representing most of the city's settlement houses. Three of the CHPC directors were also on the board of the Citizens Union. Similar overlap could be shown with the other leading civic groups in the city.

13. New York *Times*, Nov. 11, 1959, p. 37.

CHAPTER VIII. NEIGHBORHOOD ACCESS
TO THE GOVERNMENT

1. Interview with Jane Jacobs, March 14, 1963.

2. See Norton E. Long, *The Polity*, ed. by Charles Press (Chicago, Rand McNally, 1962), pp. 64–76; Wallace S. Sayre and Herbert Kaufman, *Governing New York City: Politics in the Metropolis* (New York, Russell Sage Foundation, 1960; paperback edition, New York, Norton, 1965), p. 713. COIR may be considered an example of the same phenomenon.

3. See Edward C. Banfield and James Q. Wilson, *City Politics* (Cambridge Mass., MIT Press, 1963), pp. 121–25.

4. *Ibid.*, p. 127.

5. This was implied in Mrs. Jacobs' press conference the day following the riot. See New York *Times*, Oct. 20, 1961, p. 68.

6. See David B. Truman, *The Governmental Process: Political Interests and Public Opinion* (New York, Knopf, 1951), pp. 479–

98; J. W. Peltason, *Federal Courts in the Political Process* (New York, Random House, 1955), *passim*.

7. Sayre and Kaufman, *Governing New York City*, p. 718.

8. *Ibid.*, pp. 716–19.

9. See Edward C. Banfield, *Political Influence* (New York, Free Press, 1961), *passim*.

10. Sayre and Kaufman, *Governing New York City*, pp. 715–16.

11. Nelson Polsby, *Community Power and Political Theory* (New Haven, Yale University Press, 1963), passim.

12. See Banfield, *Political Influence*, pp. 235–36.

13. Harold Kaplan, *Urban Renewal Politics: Slum Clearance in Newark* (New York, Columbia University Press, 1963), pp. 159–69.

14. See *ibid.*, p. 171.

CHAPTER IX. NEIGHBORHOOD GROUPS AND THE
PUBLIC INTEREST

1. James Q. Wilson, "Planning and Politics: Citizen Participation in Urban Renewal," *Journal of the American Institute of Planners*, XXXIX (November, 1963), 242.

2. See Martin Anderson, *The Federal Bulldozer: A Critical Analysis of Urban Renewal* (Cambridge, Mass., MIT Press, 1964), *passim*.

3. On the bases of internal democracy in private groups, see Seymour M. Lipset, *Political Man: The Social Bases of Politics* (New York, Doubleday, 1960), pp. 393–97; and Seymour M. Lipset and others, *Union Democracy: The Internal Politics of the International Typographers Union* (New York, Free Press, 1956), *passim*.

4. On the distinction, see Lipset, *Political Man*, p. 395.

5. See Wallace S. Sayre and Herbert Kaufman, *Governing New York City: Politics in the Metropolis* (New York, Russell Sage Foundation, 1960; paperback edition, New York, Norton, 1965), p. 716.

6. Martin Meyerson and Edward C. Banfield, *Politics, Planning, and the Public Interest: The Case of Public Housing in Chicago* (New York, Free Press, 1955), p. 106.

7. See Herbert J. Gans, *The Urban Villagers: Group and Class in the Life of Italian-Americans* (New York, Free Press, 1962), pp. 305–35; Jane Jacobs, *The Death and Life of Great American*

Cities (New York, Random House, 1961; paperback edition, New York, Vintage Books, 1963), *passim.;* Edward C. Banfield, *Political Influence* (New York, Free Press, 1961), p. 329.

8. Meyerson and Banfield, *Politics, Planning, and the Public Interest,* pp. 323–27.

9. The relocation program in WSURA was begun too late to be covered in this study.

10. Kaplan, *Urban Renewal Politics,* p. 16.

Index

City Planning Commission (CPC), 8,
9, 18, 21, 23-25, 26, 29, 184; and
Rockaway projects, 30, 48; and
Greenwich Village projects, 81, 96-
98, 103-04, 106, 109; and West Side
projects, 117-19, 123, 132, 135, 137-
38, 141, 143
City Planning Department (New York
City), 24, 25
Civic associations, Rockaways, 35-39,
57, 59-64
Clancy, John, 62-63, 65, 183
Cobble Hill, Brooklyn, 22, 107, 217
Coffey, Michael, 123-24, 129, 173, 181
Cohen, Myron, 136-37, 139
COIR, see Commission on Intergroup
Relations
Colored Democratic Association,
Rockaways, 38
Columbus Circle project, 113
Commission on Intergroup Relations
(COIR), 61-62, 65, 173, 181, 183-85,
190, 195; and West Side projects,
133
Committee to Save West Village
(CSWV), 10, 151, 156, 166, 171,
174-75, 185, 190, 198-201, 206-07; and
Greenwich Village projects, 85-86,
88, 93, 95, 99, 104-05
Community Council of Greater New
York, 120-21, 124, 185; Neighbor-
hood and Regional Planning Board
of, 124
Community Facilities Administration,
HHFA, 27
Community Renewal Section, CPC, 30
Community Service Society, 11, 92,
173, 184
Condemnation in urban renewal proj-
ects, 7, 8
Council for Relocation, NAACP, 64
66, 67
Council on Human Relations, 183
County leaders (New York City), 26
Courts and urban renewal, 199-204
CPC, see City Planning Commission
Crisona, Frank, 39, 47-48, 55, 60, 159
Cruise, Philip, 43, 44, 117
CSWV, see Committee to Save West
Village

Dahl, Robert, 2
Dapolito, Anthony, 90, 95, 160

Davies, J. Clarence, Jr., 10, 18, 19-21,
22, 25, 51, 64, 148, 154, 188, 190, 193-
94, 204, 207; and Greenwich Village
projects, 80-81, 83-84, 88, 90, 93, 97,
99, 103, 105, 108; and West Side
projects, 131
Democratic Club, Rockaways, 39
Democratic Party (New York City),
18, 27, 76, 99, 124, 196, 202, 205;
Reform movement in, 18, 25, 76, 99,
114-15, 125, 141-42, 144, 159-60, 165-
66
Dentler, Robert A., 2
DeSalvio, Louis, 92, 96
DeSapio, Carmine, 50, 76, 91, 102
Dobkin, Alex, 105
Dodelson, Donald, 78, 85, 221
Downtown Lower Manhattan Associ-
ation, 13
Dudley, Edward, 92-93

Edelstein, Julius, 106
Edgemere Civic Association, 49-50, 59,
170, 200
Edgemere Houses project, Rockaways, 34
87th-97th Street Business and Professional Group, 127, 171, 173-75, 187
Evans, Herbert, 217

Farbstein, Leonard, 92
FDR–Woodrow Wilson Democratic
Club, 152, 160, 165, 170, 179, 187,
197; and West Side projects, 115,
125, 129-30, 132, 136-38, 144
Federal Housing Administration
(FHA), 7, 9, 27, 46, 47
Federal National Mortgage Associa-
tion (FNMA), 27
Federation Bank and Trust Co., 16, 18
Felt, James, 17-18, 19, 21, 22, 24, 25,
188, 193-94, 207; and Rockaways
project, 54; and Greenwich Village
projects, 81, 88, 94, 97-99, 102-06;
and West Side projects, 119-20, 125,
131
FHA (Federal Housing Adminis-
tration), 7, 9, 27, 46, 47
Fingerhood, Shirley, 105
FNMA (Federal National Mortgage
Association), 27
Foley, John J., 121-25
Fox, J. Lewis, 38, 50, 55